FISHING

1977 Printing of the
1974 Edition

By Michael A. Soriano,
Technical Editor,
Garcia Corporation

BOY SCOUTS OF AMERICA
NORTH BRUNSWICK, NEW JERSEY

Requirements

1. Catch three different kinds of fish by any legal, sportsmanlike method. Identify them. (One of the fish must be taken on an artificial lure.) Clean for cooking.

2. Point out the different parts of a fly, casting, saltwater, or spinning rod. Name them. Point out the main parts of a fly, casting, saltwater, or spinning reel; or show how to take care of your fishing tackle; or tell where the chief kinds of fish are likely to be found where you live at different times of year and different times of day and in different kinds of weather.

3. Catch and identify three kinds of natural bait.

4. Give the open seasons on game fish where you live. Explain how and why they are protected by law. Tell what fish conservationists are doing to make better fishing for you.

North Brunswick, New Jersey
Library of Congress Catalog Card Number: 19-600
ISBN 0-8395-3295-4
No. 3295 Printed in U.S.A. 22M177

Contents

Let's Go Fishing

Two-thirds of the earth's surface is covered by natural bodies of water which support countless numbers of life forms. In addition, man has taken advantage of his watery planet by building innumerable holding areas for this precious natural resource in the form of recreational lakes, irrigation canals, huge power and storage reservoirs, and even tiny farm ponds. Each has its purpose in serving and preserving man; each, except for those that have been abused, has the potential to offer hours of enjoyment and excellent sport.

Fishing means many things to many people. To some, it is an occupation. To others, fishing is a relaxing escape from a daily existence of noise and familiar surroundings. Many look forward to the thrill and exciting challenge of outwitting the sly and elusive "grandpappy of them all." Whether done alone or with others, in an ocean or pond, day or night, in summer or winter — fishing can always be different and fun.

As a sport, you can participate whenever you want as long as the kind of fishing you want to do is legal. It is not the type of competition where someone must win and another lose. Even if you don't catch fish, you have still won by gaining the experience and practice for another day, or maybe you've learned something new from an experienced angler who has had some helpful advice to offer.

Fishing is an interest that can keep you busy all yearlong. Serious anglers find that there are many sidelines to the sport. As an example, you can learn to tie flies and design new patterns while studying the habits of various fish — how they live and what they eat. Learning to mount fish can be intriguing; or you can make a hobby of photographing your fishing trips. Through practice, some people have become experts in casting, catching certain types of fish, or fishing with a particular method. Many fishermen build and customize their equipment, and some even spend hours tying or designing new knots for fishing.

No one can tell you why fishing is fun. The purpose of this book is to help you understand the basic hows of fishing. Learn them and you'll be well on your way to finding out the whys for yourself.

What Is a Fish?

You'll get more out of fishing, in addition to catching more fish, if you know what they are and how they live. To start with, a fish is a cold-blooded vertebrate (an animal with a backbone) which lives and breathes in the water. Gills in the rear of a fish's mouth extract oxygen from water flowing through them and in turn transmit the oxygen to the bloodstream. Most fish have scales covering their bodies which overlap like shingles on a roof. They also have fins to propel and stabilize them in the water.

A full-grown fish never sheds its scales, and as the fish grows each scale grows larger. Their number is never increased, but if one is lost, a new one will grow to replace it. Growth is marked by rings on each scale which are quite similar to the annual growth rings on the stump of a tree. The scales are also coated with a thin skin which secretes a slimy coating. This slime reduces friction on the surface of the fish as it swims through the water. It also helps the fish to slip away from its enemies, in addition to preventing disease organisms from entering through the skin.

There is a distinct horizontal line running down the sides of many species which is called the lateral line. More than being decorative, it is a tube covering a series of nerve endings. Experiments indicate that the lateral line can detect low-frequency vibrations, helping the fish avoid underwater obstructions. It may also prove to be a sensing device which can record differences in water temperature.

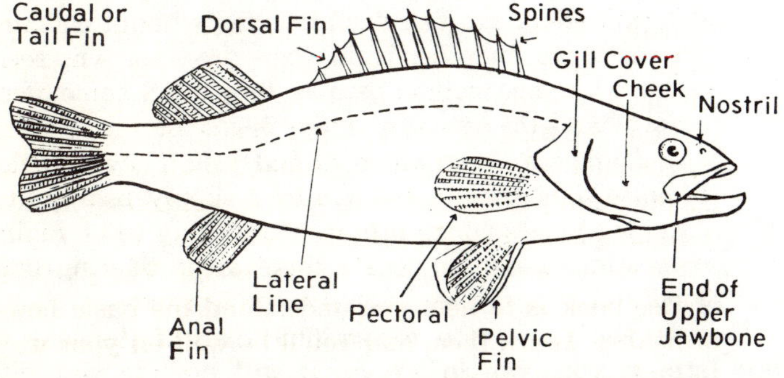

The mouths of most fish are full of tiny teeth located on their jaws, the roofs of their mouths, and, in some cases, their tongues. A few species, like carp and suckers, have no teeth at all, while others, like sharks, muskies, and barracuda, have very large teeth. These teeth are not used for chewing but, instead, to hold food. Be sure to exercise caution by using a net or gaff when landing these sharp-toothed predators.

Fish reproduce by laying eggs in a nest that is usually built by the male of the species, although sometimes the male and female work together in the construction of a nest. Once the eggs are laid, the male fertilizes them and will often stand guard until the young are safely hatched. Such is the case with bass, which will even take care of the young after they are born, and the bluegill, which may find itself guarding up to 50,000 eggs at a time. Some species, however, like the carp which will lay millions of eggs each summer, may make no special effort to protect the eggs at all.

Some biologists believe there are over 40,000 different species of fish living in freshwater and saltwater, as well as in varied extremes of temperature and altitude. Their size also varies enormously from giant whale sharks which are estimated to reach 150,000 pounds to the tiny goby fish of the Philippines which are less than 1 inch long when full grown. Of course, you won't be fishing for either of these extremes with a hook and line, but the point is that somewhere nearby you there resides at least a 1-pounder just waiting to give you a tussle and all the fun you want.

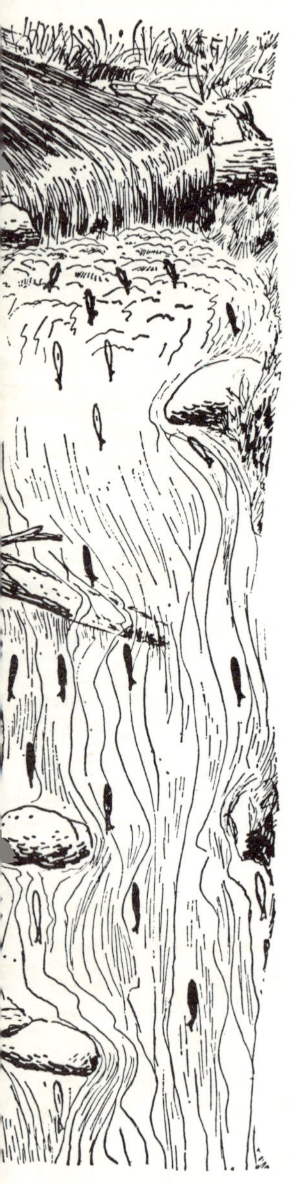

FEEDING RAINBOW

FEEDING BROWN

RESTING FISH

Locating Fish

Some fishermen, even though they have patience and determination, can fish day after day without catching anything. On the other hand, there are some who seem to have a secret method because they never come home empty-handed. Actually, there is no secret. Experienced anglers know where to find fish. They find fish because they know there is a food supply nearby and can spot places where fish are most likely to be hiding or resting. Learn to locate these areas offering both food and security, and you'll catch fish too.

If you can, get a topographic map of the lake or stream you plan to fish in. It will provide you with basic information concerning depth and the contour of the bottom. Then, ask questions. Talk to the person who rents boats or sells tackle. Local conservation agents and fishermen you meet on the water will be able to tell you the best times to fish and the kinds of natural baits or artificial lures to use which have been most productive. You'll also want to know about the water itself: Where are the sunken logs and rocks, the holes and weed beds? Where do streams flow into the main body of water? As you get answers to these questions, start to add the information to your map. As you fish the area, you'll be able to supply personal data.

Most fish activity will be found along fringe areas—around weed beds, stumps, logs, and rocks. In a stream, fish lie in front of or behind these obstructions to get away from the current and wait for food which is swept into these backwaters. In a lake, such obstructions are good hiding places for both fish and their food supply. Quiet pools in midstream or places where a stream empties into a larger body of water are likely locations for fish, since their food tends to collect in slack water. However, the nearby flowing water is comfortable for many species.

Most fish migrate according to food supplies, fluctuating oxygen levels, and changing seasons and water temperature. In the spring, fish will congregate in shallow water to feed and spawn. When the water warms up during the hot summer months, they will move into the cooler depths, returning to feed in the shallows only in the early morning and late evening hours. As the water cools again in the fall, they'll be found feeding in the shallows, only to go back to deep water again during the cold winter months.

The water temperature plays a critical role in the feeding habits of most fish. Largemouth bass, for instance, are most active when the water is 65-75 degrees Fahrenheit; smallmouth bass, on the other hand, seem to prefer their water about 5 degrees cooler. Trout generally enjoy colder water temperatures. When fishing for lake trout, the rule is to fish deep where the water temperature drops to about 40 or 50 degrees.

The key point to remember is that fish like to be near a supply of food; they also want to be able to rest and hide safely. Find places that offer these to the species you're after, and you'll find fish.

Tackle

Balanced Tackle

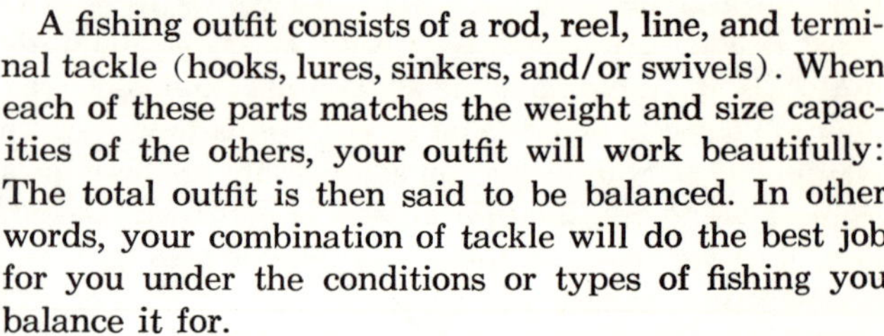

A fishing outfit consists of a rod, reel, line, and terminal tackle (hooks, lures, sinkers, and/or swivels). When each of these parts matches the weight and size capacities of the others, your outfit will work beautifully: The total outfit is then said to be balanced. In other words, your combination of tackle will do the best job for you under the conditions or types of fishing you balance it for.

If you are new to the sport, you'll be amazed at the many kinds of tackle available to choose from and the unlimited combinations that can be made to suit your personal desires in fishing equipment. If you are not sure, ask someone who knows all about tackle when selecting the different parts of your outfit. Each piece should be chosen with care to make sure it will balance with your other tackle. If you do this, your outfit will work just like you want it to for your type of fishing. Tackle that fits you and does the job always adds to the enjoyment of fishing.

When tackle is not balanced right, it can be compared to a car without shock absorbers: It may get you where you are going, but it's a bumpy, uncomfortable ride all the way. So, balanced tackle does make a difference—a big difference. In the following pages, we will investigate each of the tools of the sport in some detail to help you balance your tackle.

Fishing Rods

The majority of fishing rods (not poles) today are made from fiberglass. Although there are many different rod designs intended to perform in a variety of ways and for different situations, all rods do four vital things for the fisherman: In addition to throwing the bait during the cast or serving as a mount for the reel, a fishing rod also acts as a lever in setting the hook and playing a fish; it also serves as a cushion to protect the line from excess strain by flexing evenly to absorb various shocks and stresses while hooking, fighting, or landing a fish.

At this time it would be impossible to go into a description of all the different types, lengths, styles, weights, etc., of rods available in stores for the sportsman. But, in helping you decide, you should know that there are two basic fiberglass rod constructions: the tubular-glass rod and the solid-glass rod. Each has its good points, although the tubular-fiberglass rods of today are the most popular. The reason for this is that they are light in weight and at the same time are very strong. Also, they are unaffected by temperature changes which means they will not warp. And, in addition, a great many actions and tapers can be engineered into a tubular-glass rod.

Probably the biggest advantage of the solid-glass fishing rod is that it is easier for manufacturers to make and costs less. Unfortunately, many of the tapers and actions which anglers would like to use cannot be produced in the solid-glass rod which is heavier without additional strength than the same type rod made of tubular fiberglass. This is important to the lure fishermen who will be casting and retrieving all day long—they want a rod which handles easily and will not cause them to become tired after working a lure for an hour or two.

ROD CONSTRUCTION

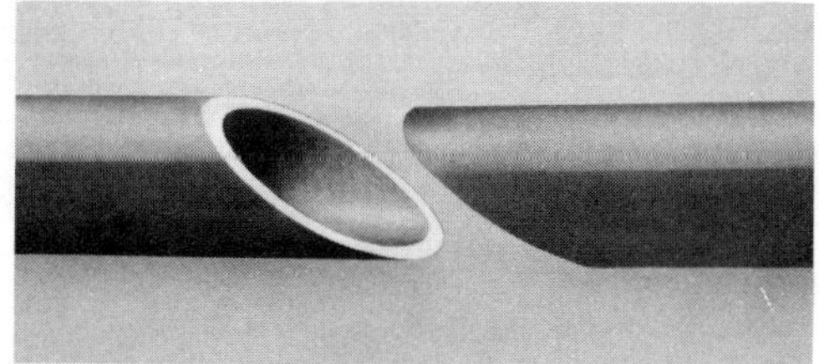

Tubular Glass

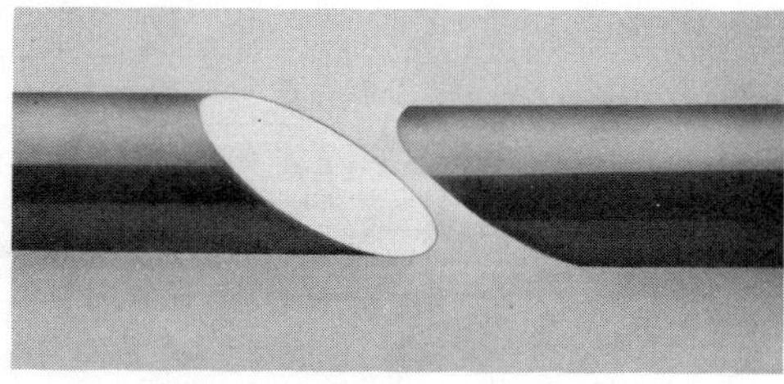

Solid Glass

GUIDES AND FERRULES

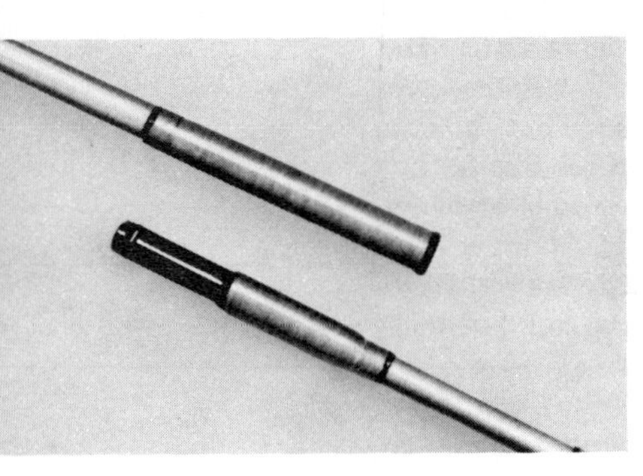

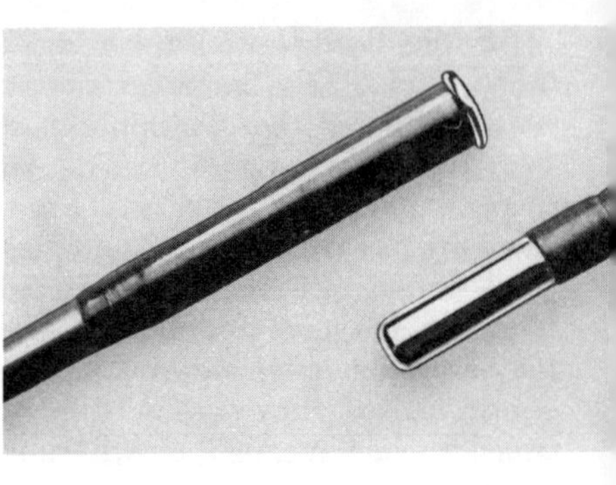

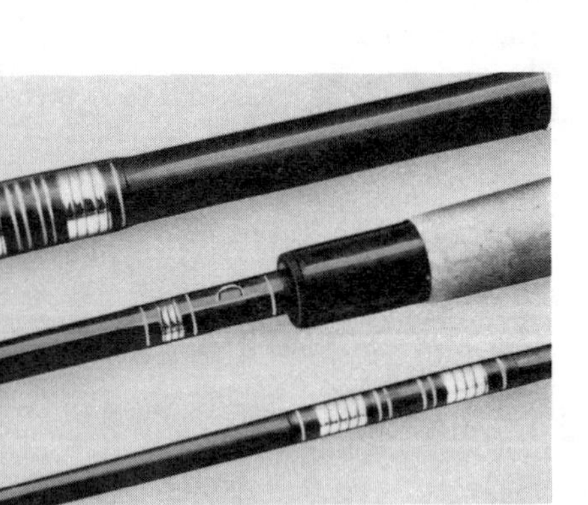

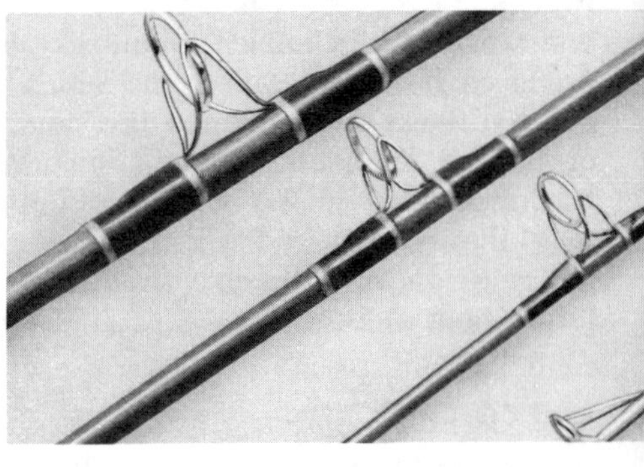

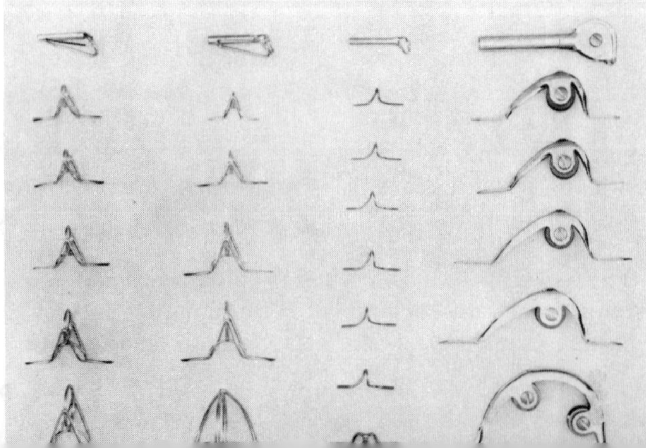

Rods are made in either one piece or in order to make them easier to transport and store, in two or more sections. For this reason, you should consider the ferrules next. Their purpose is to join the sections of a rod together to fit snugly. When the rod is taken apart, the ferrules should come apart with a pop, which tells you they have a smooth, almost airtight fit. One of the greatest enemies of a ferrule is dirt. Ferrules should be checked, cleaned, and lightly greased now and then to keep them from sticking.

There are many types of guides and tip-tops available to work in a specific way with different types of reels and fishing situations. When you cast lures or natural bait, they function as a guide to the line as it comes from the reel. During the retrieve, their purpose is to keep the line close to the rod causing the rod to bend uniformly and absorb the strain of a fighting fish. The important qualities of rod guides are that they must be smooth and very hard to protect the line and prevent line wear.

Windings and trims are used to attach guides and tip-tops to rods. Other than that, they are purely decorative and help blend the line of the ferrules to the rod. Better rods use differently colored, fine-thread windings, while others use paint for a two color effect.

Rod Handles. — Generally speaking, all fishing rods have in common major parts which should be considered in selecting a fishing rod after you have decided on your method of fishing. One part is the handle. As you can see by the illustration on page 12, although each of the rod handles is for a different type of fishing, the parts of each handle serve the same purpose in each case.

The material most often used for the foregrip and butt sections is cork, and even though all cork has holes in it, you can choose a better quality by selecting the one with the least amount of holes. By looking at the quality of the cork, you can usually judge the quality of the rod and the reliability of the manufacturer. For some special rods, wood is used; for others, they use a slip-proof, cushion-foam material. Whichever is used on the rod you would like to get, be sure it is smooth and feels comfortable in your hand.

The reel seats of most rods are made of chromed brass, chromed steel, and/or anodized aluminum. The important part of any reel seat, however, is the method used to hold the reel onto the rod. It should encompass a firm, secure locking device.

Fishing Lines

The ancestor of the modern fishing line was made from pieces of horsehair knotted together to form a strong, single strand. Eventually, possibly to prevent an era of bald horses, lines came to be made of linen

ROD HANDLES

Spin-Casting and Bait-Casting Rod

Fly Rod

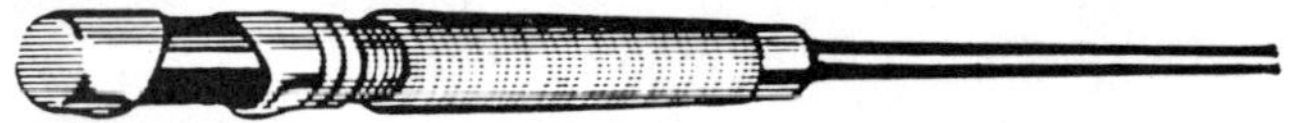

Freshwater Spinning Rod

Saltwater Spinning Rod

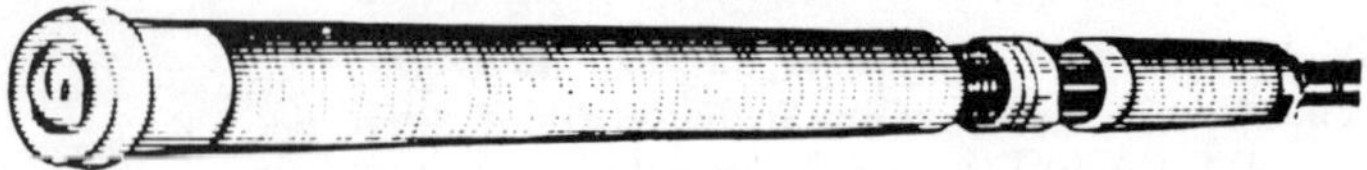

Boat and Jetty Rod

and silk. However, the problem with these materials was that they would tend to deteriorate rapidly and lose a good deal of strength in the middle of a single fishing season. The weakness would naturally show up when the line separated just as the angler hooked into a trophy-sized fish and lost a favorite lure in the process.

Because of advanced technology just before and during World War II, silk and linen were replaced by lines manufactured from synthetic materials. Today, the list of synthetic-material fishing lines includes monofilament, braided nylon, braided Dacron, nylon squidding line, wire line, and fly line (both sinking and floating).

The monofilament line is an absolute necessity on spinning and spin-casting reels because of its springiness and tendency to jump off the reel when cast. Besides having superior casting abilities, it is almost impossible to see in the water and accounts for a larger percentage of caught fish than any other type of line, making it popular among bait casters, surf casters, and trollers. The name "monofilament" gives a clue to its construction: "mono" meaning one, or single; and "filament" indicating a strand. The material used to make this line is heated and pushed out of a machine, much like toothpaste coming from the tube.

Braided lines are exactly what they imply: lengths of a particular material braided or woven together to make a single line of a certain strength. A braided nylon has a tendency to float which is quite desirable to the angler fishing a surface or semisurface lure. Since the line floats with little resistance from water pressure, the lure will respond more quickly to every life-giving twitch of the rod.

Braided Dacron, on the other hand, is very dense and heavy. It has the ability to get down deep when using deep-running plugs, jigs, and similar lures designed to make a presentation right in the fish's dining room.

The first wire lines were nothing more than plain copper wire. Today, however, the more high-priced lines are made of lead with a woven covering of nylon material. This line sinks like lead, has the ability to overcome the buoyant tendency of deep water, and can take a trolled lure down to great depths where the big ones usually are. The nylon sheath protects the soft

Weight Forward (WF)

Double Taper (DT)

Level Line (L)

lead from wear and tear, while making it possible to tie a strong knot in the line.

The modern fly line was developed as recently as 1952, although the art of fly-fishing is probably the oldest recorded method of fishing known to man. It is now produced with a center core of braided line which has a uniform strength from one end to the other and will not absorb water; a special finish is bonded to the center core which creates a definite line weight and taper. The illustration at left will give you an idea of the three basic taper designs on the market.

The level (L) line has a uniform diameter through its entire length. This is the most common line in use and is ideal for the beginner. It is not meant for distance casting; rather, it enables the novice to learn control and permits a reasonably delicate cast.

The double taper (DT) is actually two fly lines in one. Most of its length is uniform except at each end where it tapers to an identical smaller diameter. The heavier middle section aids distance casting, while the tapered ends allow a fly to drop gently onto the water. When one end has been used and begins to show signs of wear, the fisherman can simply reverse the line and begin fishing with a "new" line.

The weight forward (WF) is the perfect line for long casts and heavy-duty work in casting streamers (large flies), bugs, and poppers. It is constructed of a tapered heavy-bellied section up front which is followed by a smaller diameter running line.

In addition to tapers, fly lines are also classified as either floating or sinking. The floating line is the primary weapon of most fly-fishermen because it keeps the fly or bug on or near the surface. On the other hand, the sinking line is designed to carry the lure below the surface.

Choose the type, weight, and style of line you need for the kind of fishing you are doing.

Accessories

Leaders are connectors between the end of a line and the lure or natural bait. In some cases, when angling for sharp-toothed species like pike or muskies, a wire leader will help to keep you from losing excessive amounts of tackle and fish.

Hooks are available in many shapes, styles, and sizes. Be careful, though, not to choose one that is too large for the species of fish you are after. A fish can always swallow a hook that is too small, but a large one may scare it away. Always carry a hone or emery cloth and keep the points of your hooks in good shape. Many fish have been lost because of dull hooks.

Types of Bobbers

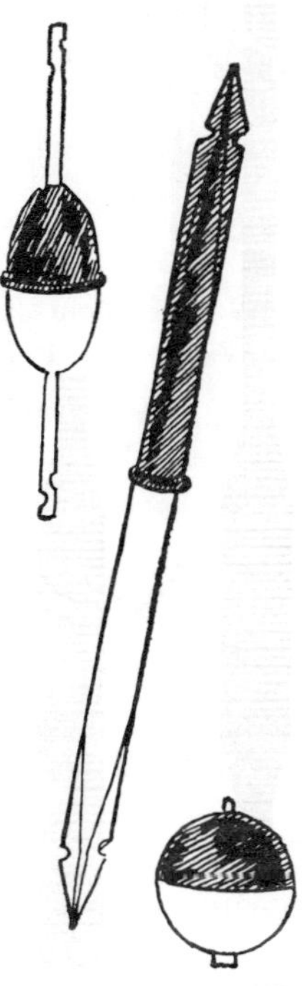

Sinkers are made in three basic styles for all-around freshwater fishing. Each style of sinker will serve the singular purpose of taking your bait down to a required depth. The bass-casting sinker is the popular style for bottom fishing, while the rubber-cored sinker is generally tied to your line when trolling. Use a split shot in any situation requiring a lightweight sinker.

Floats, or bobbers, are attached to the line and used to keep the bait suspended at a predetermined level. They also serve as warnings to fishermen that fish are toying with, or have already taken, the bait. Their coloring makes them easy to spot as they bob on the surface.

The most popular type of float is round and plastic and attaches to the line with a spring-held snap. Another popular type of float has a hole running through its center. The line is run through the hole so that the fisherman can tie a knot above the float relative to the depth at which the bait is to be held. This type of float is great when your fish will be waiting 10 to 20 feet below the surface. When you want to cast, you can reel right up to the terminal end of the rig. Casting with a snap-on float would be impossible in this situation.

Types of Sinkers

In addition to the above, there is an infinite number of accessory items designed to appeal to the fisherman, but probably the most important of all is the tackle box which should be large enough to hold whatever other items you will need to make your day's fishing successful. A set of small repair tools and lubricating oil may prove very helpful if you should have difficulty with your tackle. A hook disgorger is invaluable in removing a swallowed hook from a wriggling fish; insect repellent will protect you from annoying gnats and other pesty bugs. Carrying a set of foul-weather gear will help you cope with those famous last words, "Rain? Are you kidding? There's not a cloud in the sky!"

A landing net or gaff is a must if you are using light tackle or trying to land a good-sized fish from the water. With many fighters, you risk losing the fish as well as your tackle if you try to lift it without the aid of a net or gaff. Stream-wading fishermen – particularly trout anglers—generally carry their catches in a willow basket or canvas bag called a creel. To this waterlogged breed of angler, hip boots or waders are a must, especially when standing in swift-moving, ice-cold streams and rivers. Boat or bank fishermen use a stringer of one sort or another which can be a cord or chain run through the fish's gill and out its mouth. This will usually not harm the fish, and it can be kept alive in the water until you're ready to pack it in and go home.

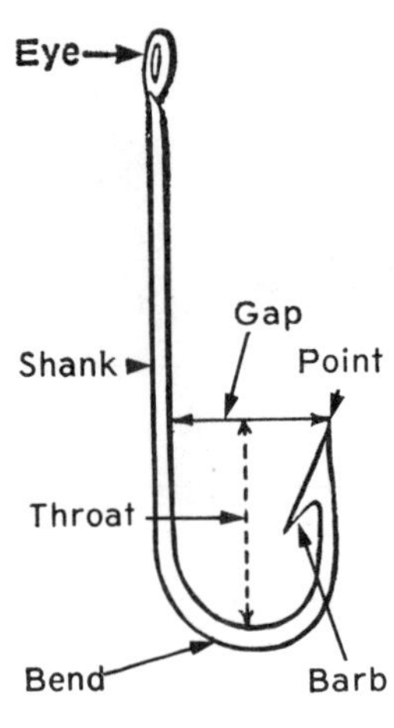

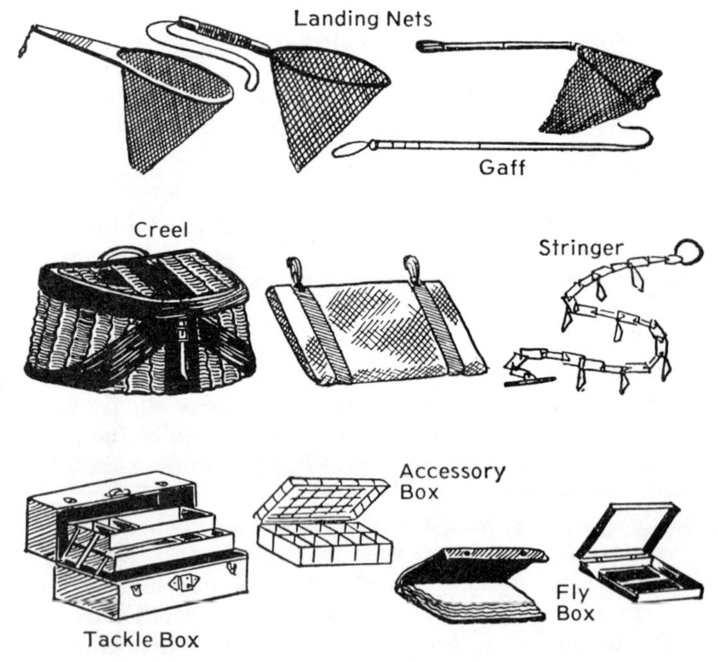

Artificial Lures

Some time before recorded history, an industrious fisherman crudely carved a chunk of wood to resemble a natural bait. He was undoubtedly thrilled when it

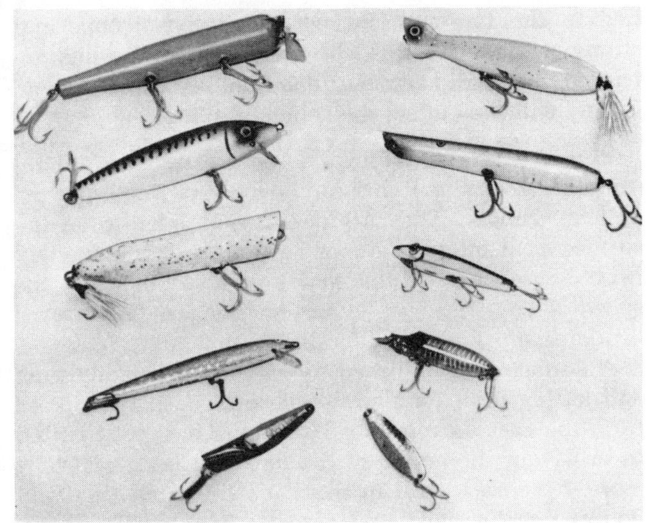

worked, and he landed the first artificially fooled fish. Since that time, anglers have been experimenting to find the perfect all-around lure that will excite fish and produce constant strikes. Artificial baits have been made from feathers, deer hair, wood, plastic, metal, and a wide variety of other materials.

Every time you visit your local tackle shop you are bound to see an artificial lure that you've never seen before. Some have been around for years, standing the test of time; others come and go because they fail the critical test of consistently producing strikes. Of the ones that do remain, there are literally thousands in the categories of fly patterns, plugs, spoons, jigs, plastic baits, and others. It is not necessary to own one of each. Experienced anglers will have selected only a few standard lures that they feel will produce the best results. Most important, they have learned how to use in the most productive manner the ones at their disposal.

The selection of properly weighted lures is another important consideration in developing a well-balanced outfit. Always choose a lure that is made to be handled by a particular rod-and-reel combination. For example, spinning tackle is designed to handle lightweight lures, while medium- or heavy-weight lures perform best with spin-casting and bait-casting tackle.

During an average day of fishing with artificial lures, you will probably want to change lures from time to time. To make matters easier, a snap swivel should be tied to the line end. Swivels are inconspicuous and strong, and in the case of lures that spin when retrieved, they will keep your line from becoming twisted. Rarely will they affect the action of a lure.

Plugs. — These artificial lures are designed to resemble a natural bait and can be made of wood, plastic, or foam rubber. They are designed to operate on the surface or at intermediate or bottom depths. Some will work at varying depths that are determined by the speed of your retrieve. The colors and design patterns available on plugs are literally innumerable.

A surface plug is fished by casting to a likely area and letting it sit for a while (usually until the ripples from the cast disappear). Then, give it a good twitch to bring out the action of the lure and let it sit some more. Be sure to reel in the slack line each time you do this.

Surface Plugs

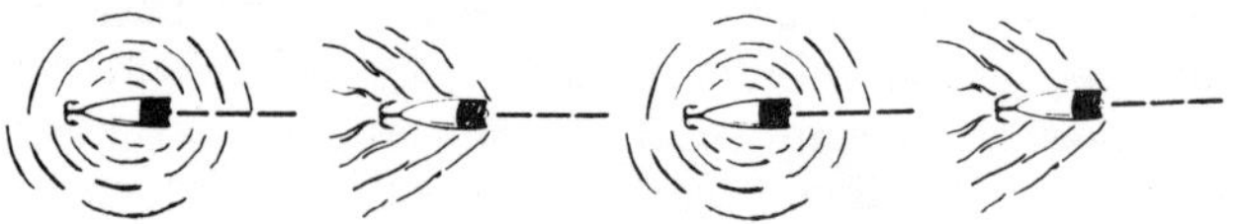

A subsurface plug has a small lip in front which causes it to dive and wiggle when reeled in. To work properly, it should be reeled in, letting it dive and wiggle, and then stopped, allowing it to rise to the surface. Let it rest for a few seconds and repeat the procedure.

Deep Running Plugs

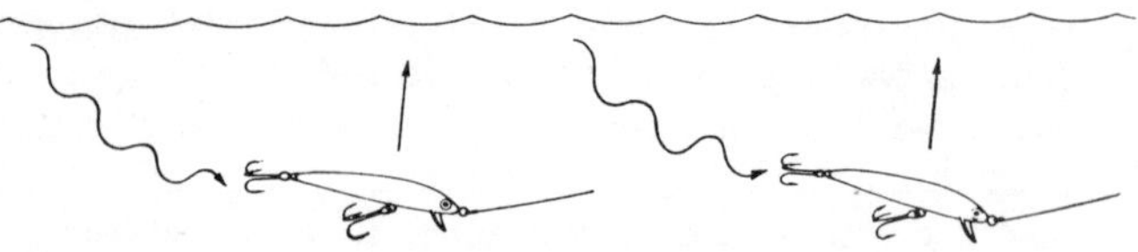

A deep-running plug has an exaggerated lip on the front end. To work one properly, simply cast it out and reel it in rapidly, causing it to dive down deep.

A sinking plug will go straight to the bottom when it is cast. No matter how slow or fast you reel in, it will stay on or near the bottom.

Jigs. — Also known as lead heads, these are simply a hook with a molded piece of lead near the hook's eye. They should be jerked through the water in a series of short movements. The advantage of jigs is in their ability to get way down deep.

Jigs

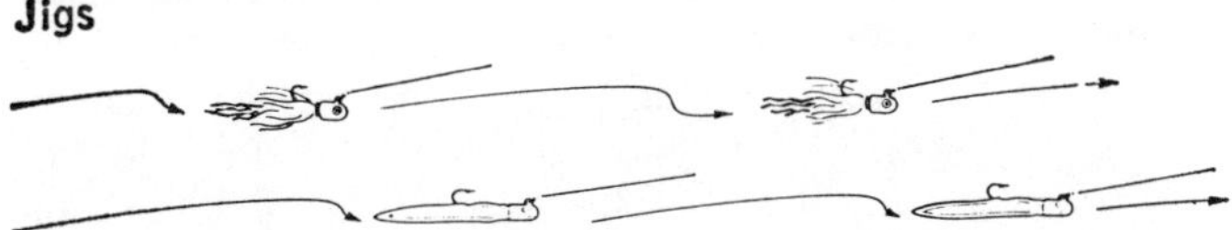

Spoons and Wobblers.—As the name suggests, spoons are shaped much like the bowl of an ordinary tablespoon with, of course, a hook attached. When trolled or retrieved, they have an enticing side-to-side sparkling action. The basic design of a wobbler is similar to the spoon's. The difference is that wobblers are usually painted in a wide variety of colors, whereas spoons are either silver, chromed, or gold plated.

An erratic retrieve is usually the most productive method of fishing them. Give the lure a healthy pull, let it flutter toward the bottom, and then pull again. Each time, remember to reel in the slack line.

Spoons and Wobblers

Spinners. — This artificial lure has a revolving blade attached to a center shaft through the lure. The attraction of a spinner is the swirling, flashing blade which draws the attention of the fish. In order for it to function properly, it must naturally be drawn through the water. Retrieve it for a short distance, let it flutter downward, and repeat the technique.

Spinners

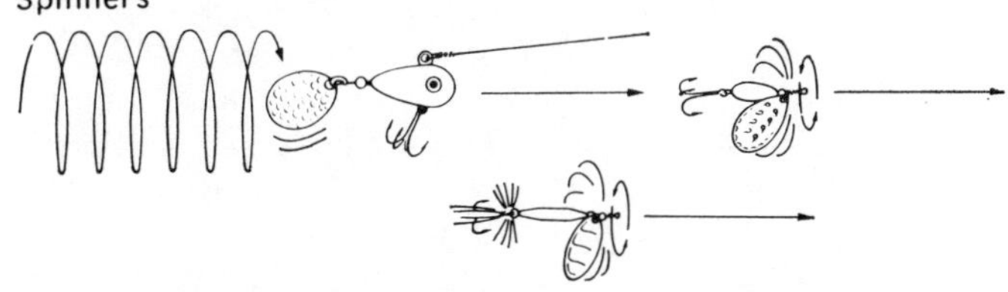

Plastic Worms. — Probably the deadliest, all-time big bass catcher so far is the plastic worm. When it was first introduced in the 1950's, not many people were sure what to do with it, so it was just another lure — that is, until recently. The trick to fishing with the worm is essentially the same as with any other artificial lure. It is up to the fisherman to impart a tantalizing, lifelike action to the hunk of plastic on the end of the line. Some fishermen prefer to cast and reel, twitching the rod tip every now and then, causing the worm to undulate exotically. Others find that an extremely slow retrieve causing the worm to "crawl" across the bottom is an effective method.

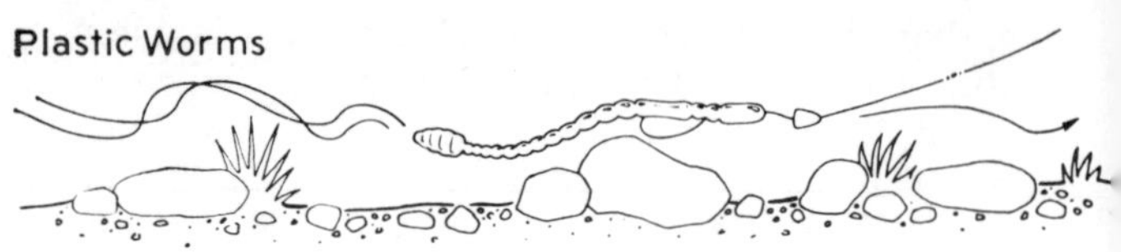

Natural Baits

Generally speaking, you can use anything for bait that a fish will eat. Experienced fishermen, however, always insist on the freshest bait possible and usually prefer to obtain it in the surrounding area of the spot they plan to fish. They find that it is best to offer fish what they want and to duplicate the natural food that is available at the moment.

Earthworm

Night crawlers are probably the most popular fishing worms, measuring 8 to 12 inches long when stretched out. You can find them at night on fairly wet ground if you walk carefully and quietly, using a flashlight to spot them. Golf courses, baseball fields, or even your front lawn are good places to hunt.

Ordinary *earthworms* are easier to get. Just dig them up in a garden area or find them under logs, rocks, and piles of weeds or grass. To be sure you always have a supply of worms make a compost pile from grass clippings and leaves. Or keep a plot of ground soaked with greasy or soapy water.

Crayfish Tail

In many places, *crayfish* are rated as one of the best baits for big bass. Catch them by placing a small-mesh net across the riffles of a stream and then going upstream overturn rocks and stones. Before hunting for crayfish, be sure it is a legal practice. Some states have a closed season on taking them.

Live *hellgrammites* are also excellent natural baits for bass. Because they are tough, they can be cast over and over again without coming off the hook. You'll find them in swift, rocky riffles. As with crayfish, hellgrammites can be caught by using a net setup downstream. However, be careful when you pick one up. The powerful jaws they use for holding onto rocks and logs in a swift current can inflict a nasty bite; clip them off as well as the claspers on their tails.

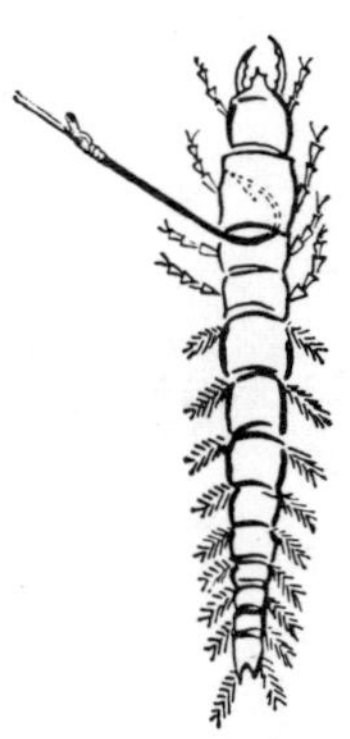
Hellgrammite

Shiners are favorite minnow baits with both fish and fishermen. Carefully hooked through the lips or behind the dorsal fin, they will stay alive on the hook for quite a while. Dead, they work well with bottom feeders such as catfish. They can be seined or dip-netted from many areas, but keep in mind that many states have laws to protect them during the spawning season. In addition, it may be illegal to fish with them in many states or areas, as is the case with carp and suckers.

Knots for Fishing

Ways To Hook a Minnow

Contrary to the thinking of many novice fishermen, a simple overhand knot will not do in most fishing situations. Although a knot may seem insignificant and hardly noticeable to the observer, it can be, and quite often is, the crucial factor between success and failure. Before we proceed, make a mental note of these elementary considerations when tying any knot: Knots should be tied carefully and then drawn up tightly in one smooth motion; when turns in and around the line are called for, make five or more of those turns to ensure the strongest knot possible; and finally, test each knot you tie with a steady pull. Weak knots will result in lost fish.

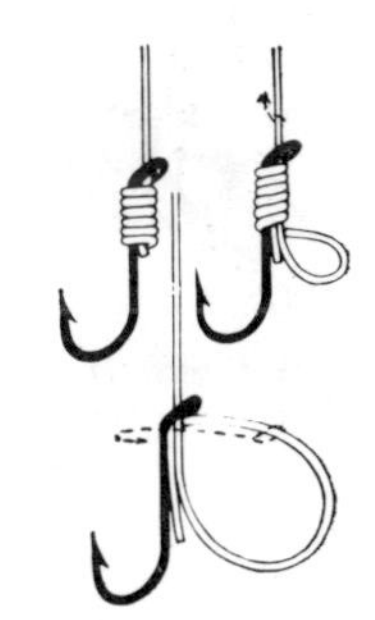
Snelling a Hook

Snelling a Hook.—A neat and simple way of attaching a hook to monofilament for certain types of bait fishing. To make a double-gang hook rig leave the free line end long and tie in a second hook behind the first. This is a popular way of hooking worms for trolling or drifting.

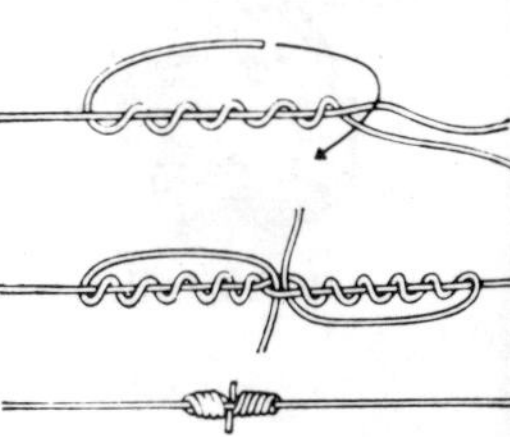
Blood or Barrel Knot

Blood or Barrel Knot. — Usually used to join two strands of monofilament together. Lap the ends of the lines or leaders several inches. Then twist one around the other, making at least five turns. Place the end between the strands and hold them together between thumb and forefinger. Wind the same number of turns (five) in the opposite direction, using the end of the other line. Then pull on the two ends to draw the turns closer together. When they have closed up snugly, pull tight on the ends to make the knot as small as possible. Clip the ends.

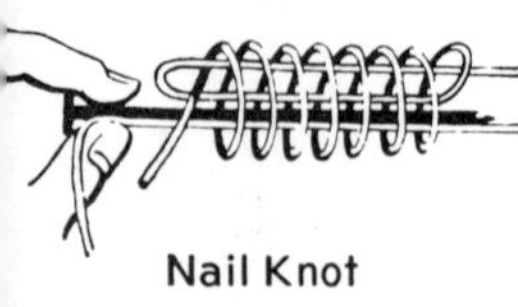
Nail Knot

Nail Knot. – This is a good way of tying monofilament to lead-core line or backing to a fly line. First, position the nail (or any similar object) along the lead core. Then lay a loop of monofilament on the nail. With the free end of monoline, take five or six turns over that loop and the nail and lead core, as shown. Next, run the end of the mono through the loop. Tighten the knot by pulling on both lines, slip the nail out, and tighten the knot all the way. Clip the protruding ends short.

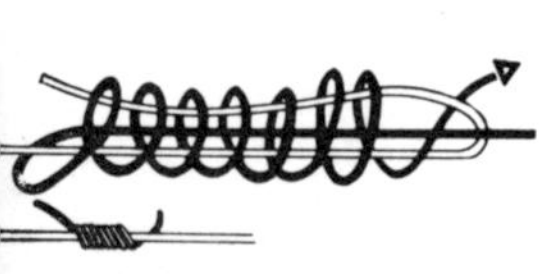
Wire Line To Mono Knot

Wire Line to Mono Knot. – Holding the wire line in your left hand, fold 4 inches of the end back over the standing part of the line. Run monofilament through the middle of the bend in the wire passing it behind the wire and then over it. Make seven close turns around both lines. Pass the end of the mono over the center strand of monofilament and under the top strand of the wire, and then draw up snugly. Cutting the free end of the wire would leave a burr that can cut fingers. Instead, bend it back and forth. It will break close to the turns of the monofilament, leaving no burr.

Putting Line on Spool

Putting Line on Spool. – Securing fishing line, monofilament or braided, is quick and easy with this method. Begin by tying a simple overhand knot at the end of the line, snipping the excess line close to the knot. Pass the line around the spool and form a loop beneath the line at A and B. Bring the free end over B and then down through the loop. The overhand knot prevents the loops from slipping through each other as the line is drawn tightly around the spool.

Turle Knot

Turle Knot. – This knot is popular with Atlantic salmon fishermen. The turle knot makes a straight connection between the hook shank and leader.

Begin by passing the end of the leader through the hook's eye from the front; then slide the fly up the leader so it will be out of the way.

Make a slipknot in the end of the leader by bringing the free end around twice, like a double overhand knot.

Draw the knot tight and pass the loop over the fly as shown. Pull the leader and manipulate the loop so that it tightens around the back of the hook's eye and *not* in the eye or on the leader itself.

Spinning

The technique of spin fishing, or spinning, was developed in Europe before World War II. It was the spinning reel which was the determining factor between spin fishing and other methods of rod-and-reel angling popular at the time. The spool (the line-storage area) of this type of reel does not turn when an artificial lure or natural bait is cast. Instead, line is pulled from the spool only by the forward momentum of the lure's weight while the line spool remains stationary. Thus, there are no moving parts during the cast, and the line is relatively free from resistance as it travels away from the reel. To the fisherman, this meant longer, more effortless casts; and, in addition, it was less possible to develop a backlash or tangle of line with the spinning reel because line would stop coming off the spool at the same time the lure hit the water. With other methods, the line spool would continue to turn releasing line, but there was no place for it to go once the lure was in the water. Consequently, the line would loosen, tangle, and knot up.

Following the war, spinning was introduced into the United States and has since swept across the country to become the most popular method of fishing with many Americans. A large number of anglers feel that a spinning outfit is by far the most versatile combination of fishing equipment they own because it performs equally well with a variety of natural-bait and artificial-lure sizes. When it comes to casting distance, the spinning rod and reel has no equal in surf or stream. To the beginner, spinning is the easiest type of tackle on which to learn the fundamental techniques of fishing.

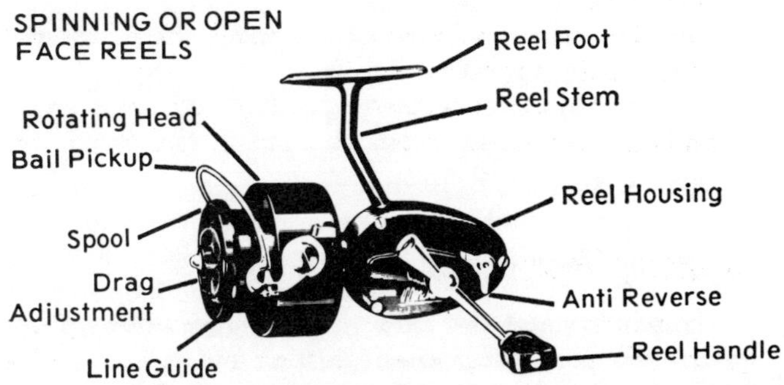

Spinning Reels

To the fishermen using them, all spinning reels operate on the same basic principle. As we go through the steps, look at the photo on page 23 and locate each of the parts we explain to help you understand how a spinning reel works.

The **spool** is the line-storage area of any reel. During the cast it does not move at all; in fact, as opposed to other types of reels, the spool of a spinning reel never rotates during casting or retrieving. When you cast, line is pulled off the stationary spool by the weight of the lure.

When fishermen want to retrieve line, they turn the **handle** which causes the line to wind around the spool by means of the **rotating head,** which revolves around the spool, and the **line guide** which guides line onto the spool. We said earlier that the spool never revolves during casting or retrieving, and it doesn't. However, it does move in and out during the retrieve which causes the line to be distributed evenly onto the spool. The only time the spool itself rotates is when a fish pulls and activates the **drag.** The drag adjusts to offer resistance while a fighting fish pulls line from the reel; it helps fishermen to keep their tackle from being strained unnecessarily and their line from being broken.

The features you should look for in selecting a good spinning reel are as follows:

- The reel housing is corrosion resistant.
- Lubricating parts are easy to get at.
- The handle folds for protection, and the grip is comfortable.
- An anti reverse prevents the handle from turning backward, which allows anglers a free hand to land their fish.
- The line guide is made of a smooth, hard material (preferably tungsten carbide).
- The gear system operates smoothly with an even in-and-out movement from the spool (for even line winding).

10 O'CLOCK

You're comfortable and relaxed. You have the lure in position, pickup bail out of the way, and reel ready for casting. You are concentrating on the target.

Spinning Techniques

This is fun and also rather simple if you think about what you are doing when starting out. Once you've gotten your outfit together, practice casting a bit before going out to your local fishing hole. To start, attach a weight or casting plug (without hooks) to the line end and let it hang about 6 inches from the tip-top. Then, holding the rod firmly in your casting hand, as illustrated on these pages, place two fingers in front of the reel stem and two in back of it and let your thumb rest comfortably on top of the rod.

Prepare to cast by holding the outfit firmly, but don't strangle the rod—just relax. Point the index finger of your casting hand down toward the line, and hook the line with your fingertip just in front of the reel's bail. As you continue to hold the line with your fingertip, reach down with the thumb and index finger of your free hand and move the bail across the face of the reel until it clicks into the open position. That's it! You're all ready for your first cast. Don't squeeze the line with your finger; just use enough pressure to keep the line from falling off the reel spool. Let's move on now and take a look at the casting technique.

Before you make your first cast, picture yourself standing in and facing the center of a clock. Using the rod as the hour hand, point the tip at 10 o'clock. The cast should follow in one smooth continuous motion bringing the rod tip from 10 o'clock to 1 o'clock and then back again to 10 o'clock—let the rod do all the work. Then, review the illustrations on these pages. You simply control the power which has been built into it. Practice this suggested action a little before letting go of the line. Use your forearm in a chopping action to make the casting motion, and you'll be able to feel all the power developed by the rod as it returns to the starting position.

When the rod is returned to the 10 o'clock position, the line should be released immediately from your fingertip. With practice, you'll soon learn exactly when to release the line for a perfect cast. However, don't be discouraged with your first attempts. If you remember two basic rules for spin casting you'll be able to cast correctly in no time: (1) If the cast goes into a high arcing flight, you are releasing the line too soon; (2) if the lure splashes into the water at your feet, the line is being released too late.

1 O'CLOCK

Note that, while your hand has started the return of the rod handle toward "10 o'clock," the rod tip and lure are still going back. Here is the power for your cast. Don't waste it by stopping at "1 o'clock."

10 O'CLOCK

Let go of the line here. Your first few casts may go almost straight up. If so, you are releasing the line too soon—a natural error if you have been casting by slower methods.

Bait Casting

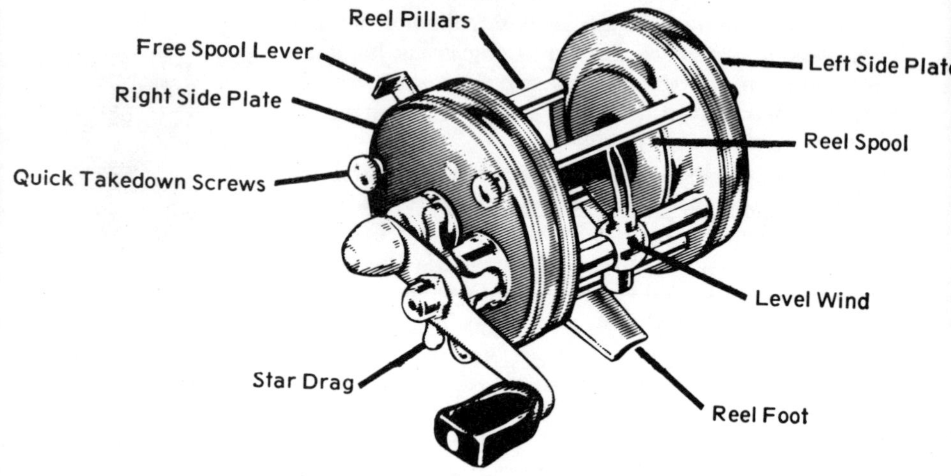

Reels

The operating principle of the bait-casting (conventional) reel has not changed since its development in the early 19th century. Modern improvements and machine skills, however, have made today's bait-casting reel far better than its earlier models. The term "bait casting" comes from early days when the reel was used to cast live minnows.

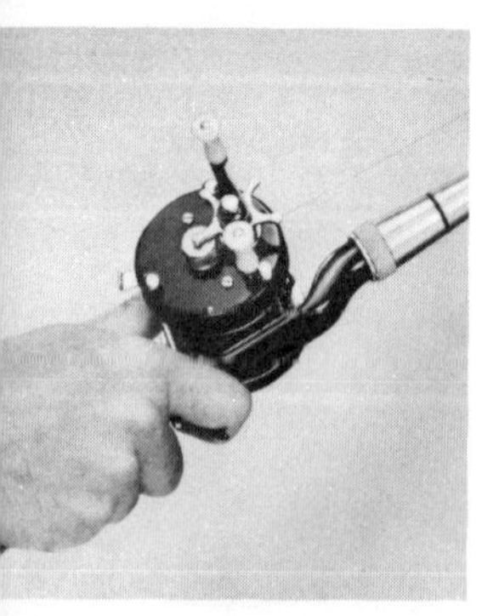

Grip handle firmly, reel handles on top

The revolving-spool reel, as the bait-casting reel has also been called, is somewhat more difficult to master than the fixed-spool (spinning) reel. Once the lure hits the water after a cast, line can come off the reel, for the spool continues to rotate unless it is controlled by the angler. Lacking practice in line control, the newcomer may spend more time unknotting backlashed line than fishing.

Nevertheless, many fishermen today prefer the bait-casting outfit for a number of reasons. Bait-casting tackle tends to have the oomph and backbone required for fishing in areas of heavy weed growth and underwater obstructions. In addition, once the casting technique is perfected, quite a few anglers insist that more accurate casts are possible with the old conventional-styled reel than with any other type of tackle.

You can judge a good bait-casting reel by looking for these features:

- A comfortable and well-balanced handle
- An easily adjustable drag (which not all conventional reels have)
- An antibacklash system to help control each cast
- A free-spool system to disengage the gears for long casts
- A level wind for even line spooling on freshwater models
- Precision engineering for minimum space between spool and sides to prevent monofilament line from getting behind the spool
- Strong, corrosion-resistant material construction of side plates
- Quick takedown features which make changing line spools and maintenance easier.

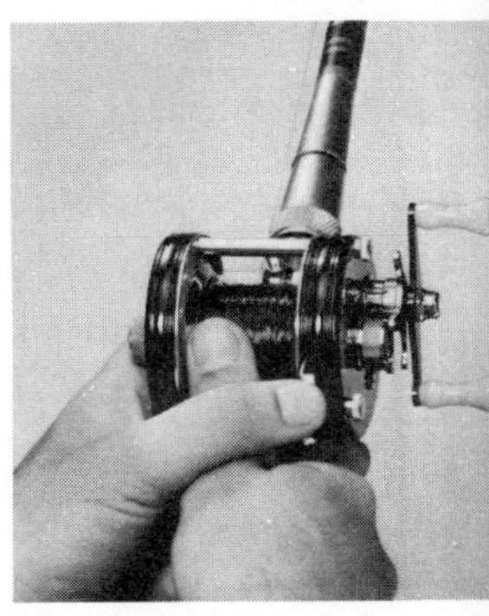

Press free spool button

Bait-Casting Techniques

As is true of all casting techniques, the key to good bait casting is timing, not power. When you first start to cast, forget about distance; apply your concentration to the perfection and control of the basic skills that follow. See illustrations on these pages.

Prepare for the cast by holding the rod grip firmly with the handles of the reel on top. The rod butt should be in a straight line with your forearm. Rest your thumb on the edge of the reel spool with some pressure directly on the spool itself.

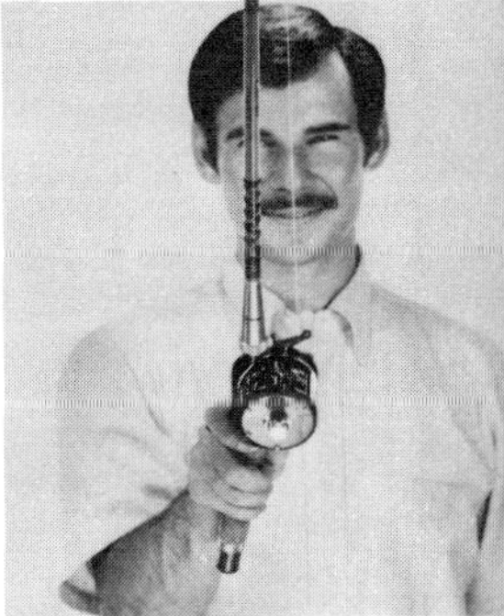

Get ready and aim

Before each cast, press the free spool release button while continuing to keep the line from unwinding. (Once the cast is completed, a turn of the handle will give you line control again.)

You are now ready to attempt your first cast. Bring the rod up in line with your aiming eye. The rod butt should continue to be parallel (as illustrated) with your forearm and should point directly at your elbow.

The casting action with this type of tackle should be the same as the smooth continuous 10 o'clock – 1 o'clock–10 o'clock method described in the "Spinning" section. As the rod returns to the 10 o'clock position, release *some* of the thumb pressure on the reel spool. As the bait nears the target, apply pressure gently and "set" the bait down on the water. For additional control of the reel's spool rotation, consult the manufacturer's instructions for brake adjustments.

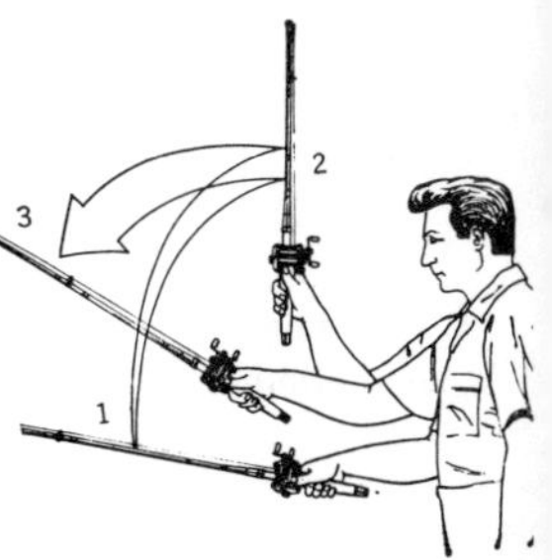

Use the rod's power

Spin Casting

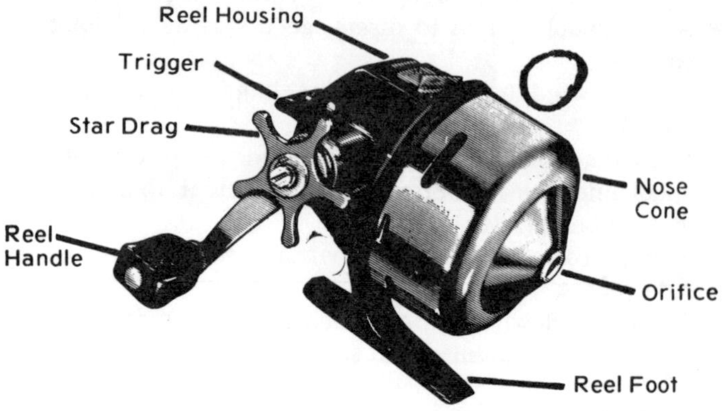

Reels

The spin-casting (close-faced) reel is very closely related to the spinning reel. In fact, it is a spinning reel but with a covered line spool. When the spin-casting reel was first introduced, it tried to encompass the best features of the spinning reel and the conventional bait-casting reel. However, the original design of the reel bothered many fishermen for some reason. Eventually, an ingenious American fisherman came up with the idea of covering up the moving parts of the reel by putting a metal shroud over the front end. This left the handle as the only visible moving part. Thus, the closed-faced spinning reel of today is truly an American invention.

When selecting a spin-casting reel, look for these features:

- A corrosion-resistant reel housing
- Easy-to-get-at lubricating parts
- An easy-to-operate and comfortable push button which replaces opening the bail and holding the line on a spinning reel
- A smooth-working gear system with a constant in-and-out movement of the line spool so line is distributed evenly (not all spin-casting reels have this type of spool)
- An easily adjustable and conveniently located drag which works smoothly over a wide range of settings
- A smooth, hard-material orifice (opening) in the nose cone to prevent too much line wear.

Spin-Casting Techniques

The spin-casting reel is mounted on the same type of rod as the conventional, or bait-casting, reel and in the same manner—on top. The step-down reel seat makes it much easier for the angler to reach and control the thumb trigger which plays a vital role in casting with this reel.

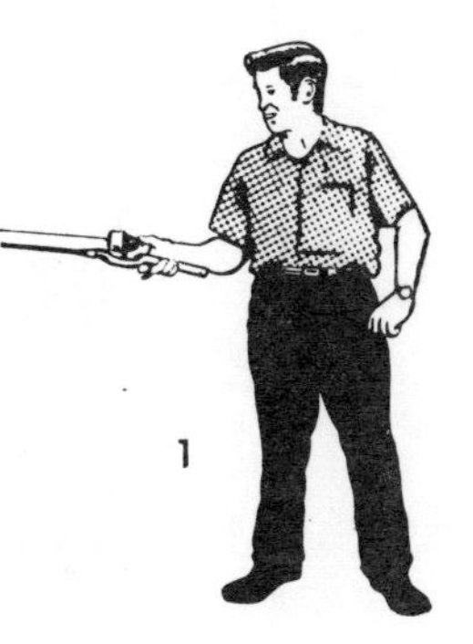

1

Your first step in fishing with the spin-casting outfit is to prepare for the cast which is simplest with a spin-casting reel. Just follow these four basic steps:

1. Hold the rod comfortably in your casting hand, remembering that the reel should be on top of the rod.
2. Reel the lure in so that it hangs about 6 or 8 inches below the rod's tip-top.
3. Now that the rod and reel are ready for casting, tilt the entire outfit so that the reel handle is on top and your knuckles are on top. This manner of holding the outfit will give you freedom of wrist movement for adding an extra snap to each cast.
4. Rest the thumb of your casting hand on the casting trigger of the reel. Push the trigger down with your thumb and hold it there.

2

Now, let's take a look at the cast itself, see illustrations. Actually, the motions and technique are almost exactly the same as described earlier in the section on spinning. Start the cast by holding the rod in the 10 o'clock position, remembering to keep the casting trigger depressed. Then, with a smooth, steady wrist/forearm motion bring the rod tip back to 1 o'clock, again keeping that trigger pressed in. Once the rod tip is up, flexing and straining with power, bring it back to the starting 10 o'clock position immediately. Now is the time to take your thumb off the casting trigger and allow the line to fire out toward your target. Don't be discouraged if your first casts are not perfect. A few practice casts should help you develop the proper coordination, and soon you'll be casting like a pro.

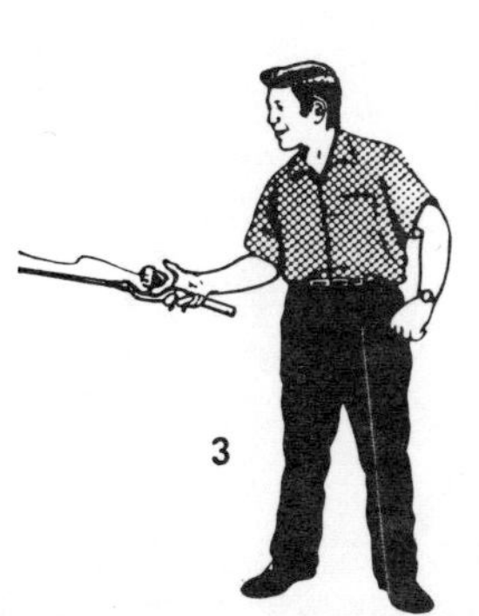

3

Fly-Fishing

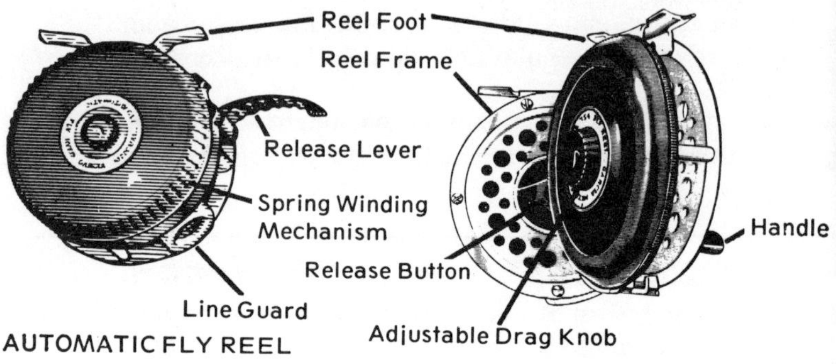

Fly-fishing is probably the world's oldest recorded method of angling. A book written in A.D. 300 called *De Natura Animalum* contains a chapter referring to "a unique method of angling in Macedonia." The fishermen of those early days of fly-fishing began to dress up hooks to look like insects which, they noticed, the local fish were eating. In addition to these "insects," the early fishermen found that using a light, limber rod also made catching supper more exciting, adding fun to chores. Eventually, fishing began to take on the aspects of a game, and fishermen started using both lighter rods and line.

Fly-fishing, as we know it today, emerged as the most artistic and challenging form of the sport. Fly-fishermen consider catching fish relatively minor to perfecting their presentation and knowledge of fly patterns. There are two major categories of flies which concern them: wet flies, which sink slowly in the water and resemble a drowned or an underwater insect or minnow; and dry flies, which float on the surface like an insect that has perhaps just dropped into the water from overhanging foliage.

Reels

The fiy reels used in today's sport are the single action, the multiplying, and the automatic. Their difference is primarily a matter of mechanism, which is implied in their names: The multiplying fly reel has a fast-retrieve gear ratio while the single action does not, and the automatic reel takes up line by merely touching a trigger which activates a spring-loaded mechanism.

The operating principle, however, is the same for all of them. Their major functions are (1) to store the line while fishing, (2) to control the fish after it is hooked, and (3) to act as a counterweight to the very long-tipped fly rod.

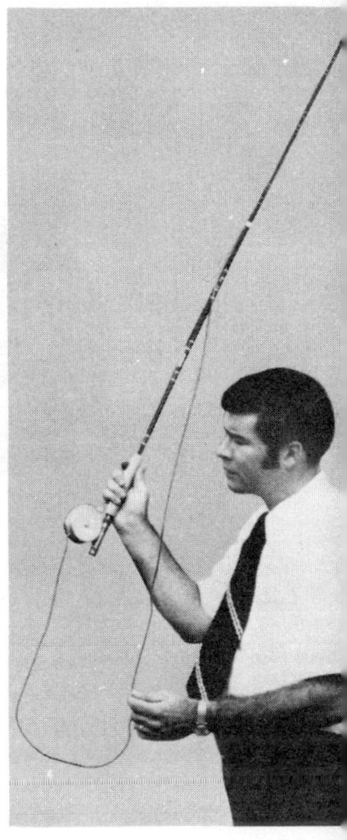

Fly-Fishing Techniques

Half the excitement of fly-fishing, or fly rodding, is in the art of casting. After practicing the technique, you'll enjoy making a proper presentation even when there are no fish around. Let's take a closer look at this method of outwitting fish.

Fly-casting is nothing more than applying positive, smooth power to a rod through timing and rhythm. Your size or strength has nothing to do with your ability to cast. The best place to start is at a nearby park or on your front lawn. Tie a small fly on the end of the leader, and you'll be able to follow the action of the line and fly more easily. For safety sake, however, clip the hook off the fly while you are in the process of practicing.

There are three distinct parts to every cast with a fly-fishing outfit: the pickup, the backcast, and the forward cast. The pickup and the backcast are basic to successful casting. Once you put your mind to it, you'll see that they are relatively easy to learn.

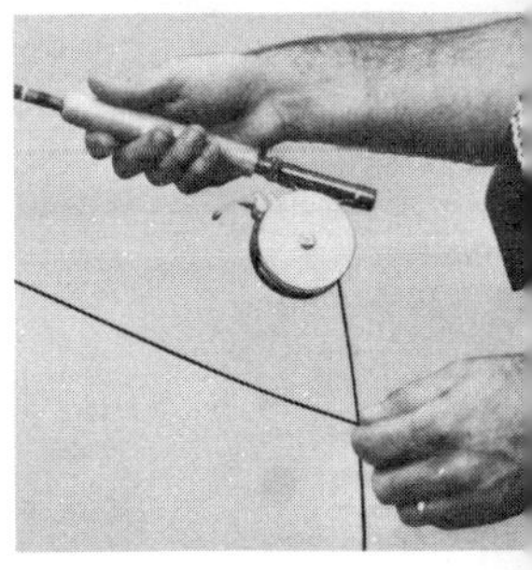

The Pickup. — Stretch out about 30 feet of fly line on the grass in front of you. With the reel and guides underneath the rod, point the tip of the rod directly at the fly at the end of the line. Grasp the line between the reel and the rod's first guide with your free hand. Separate your feet and stand comfortably. Now, turn 45 degrees in the direction of your casting hand. This will allow you to follow the motion and action of the line while making the cast.

Start the line coming toward you by lifting your arm up and back in a smooth action (position 1 of the illustration). Don't let the line in your left hand slip through your fingers. The idea is to throw the line up

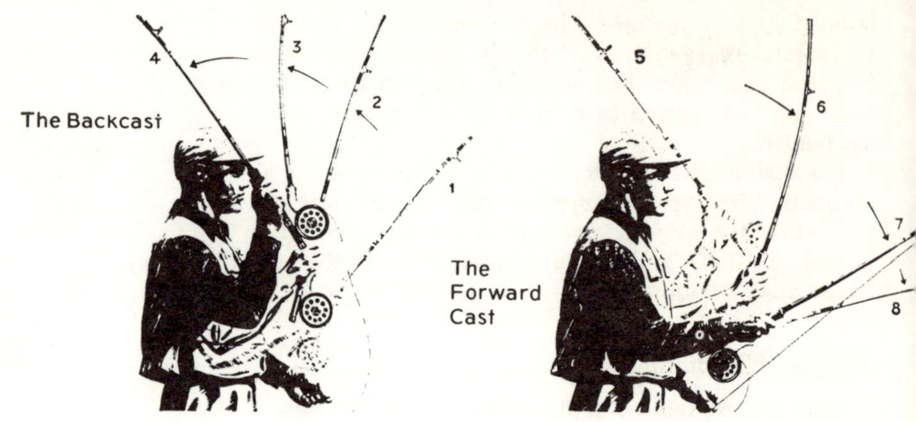

and behind you toward the sky. In position 2 the rod is at full power, pulling the line at maximum acceleration.

The Backcast. — When the rod is vertical, stop the power and flick your wrist backward and upward. Keep an eye on the line: It should loop behind you and begin to straighten. Now, all you have to do is pause momentarily until the line completely straightens and you feel a slight tug. A common fault is starting the forward cast before the line is straight which deprives the cast of the power you want. Remember that all-important pause, if you wish to be a good fly caster.

The Forward Cast. — Once you have completed the backcast, including the pause with the line straight out in back of you, all that remains is to bring your arm and the rod forward. Start slowly, and increase the speed steadily. If you take your time and don't rush the cast, you'll find it easy and natural.

Leader Construction

Leaders serve as a connecting link between the line and lure. Attached to the fly-line end, a leader will transmit the power of the cast to the fly and cause it to "turn over," landing gently on the surface of the water.

The majority of fly rodders prefer a tapered leader because of superior casting qualities. Standard leader lengths measure from 7½ to 9 feet. However, the longer the leader the more difficult the cast. Attach the thicker "butt section" of the leader to the line with a nail knot (see page 22).

Freshwater Fish

Bass

The **black bass** is about the most popular freshwater fish in the United States. It has probably seen and turned its nose up at every type of natural bait and artificial lure ever made. This bass reminds us that, except for remote wilderness areas, average fishermen must be thoroughly familiar with their tackle, natural baits, artificial lures, and abilities to catch its wary interest. Almost all bass, both young and old, are unpredictable and do not feed all day long. An old bass has learned its lesson through experience and is difficult to fool.

You may wonder why there is so much interest in a fish as unpredictable as the black bass. You will continue to wonder until the day when you are working a surface lure along the shoreline of a calm, peaceful cove and all of a sudden your calm day is shattered by the thunderous lunge of a black bass. Your line will peel off the reel with your drag singing, and you'll think your tackle will never stand the strain when the bass makes its first spectacular leap in an effort to shake the hooks from its mouth. This is when you must be careful, because the bass knows all the tricks in the book. When it runs, let it have all the line it needs to tire itself out. But watch out when it heads for underwater logs, brush, or rocks that can hopelessly tangle your line. When it doubles back heading straight for you, reel like mad to take up that slack and keep tension on the line. Finally, when the bass tires and you've reeled it up close, don't be surprised if it tries one last leap for freedom. Just keep that line taut and carefully slip a net over its head.

The **largemouth bass** is the most popular bass mainly because it is found in almost any state. It has been introduced to many farm ponds, larger lakes, reservoirs, and slow-moving rivers. The largemouth varies in color but typically has a dark-green, brown, or black coloring on its back, with lighter green sides and a gray or pale-yellow belly. The lateral line is a wide, broken band which runs from cheek to tail, and the jawline extends beyond its eye. The largemouth bass grows to about 8 pounds in the Northern States and to a record 22 pounds 4 ounces in the South where it has a longer growing and feeding season.

The **smallmouth bass** prefers colder water temperatures and cleaner water conditions than its cousin, the largemouth; hence, its distribution throughout the country is limited. Although its size is considerably smaller in rivers (where a 2- to 3-pounder is a bruiser), it can grow from 6 pounds to the record 11 pounds 15 ounces in colder lakes. The smallmouth generally puts up a bigger battle, which includes quite an acrobatic display, than the largemouth.

The body coloring of the smallmouth bass varies from pale yellow to dark brown, depending on its habitat. Usually, it appears olive gold with a luster of metallic bronze, highlighted by red eyes and a creamy-white to gray underbelly. Its lateral line is made up of distinctive dark bars or bands running along its sides. The jaw of the smallmouth extends back only to the middle of its eye.

Once you have found out that a certain stretch of water contains black bass, locating them is not nearly as difficult as trying to get them to feed on your natural bait or lure. If the largemouth is your quarry, keep in mind that it likes warmer water with weeds and a mud bottom or warm, sluggish rivers. Then try to locate the places it likes which are typically fishy, offering shade and cover.

The river smallmouth likes water that is cool, fast, and clean. You'll find it along the river's rocky stretches lying behind, beneath, or within the depressions between rocks and boulders. In a lake, the smallmouth will gather along rocky shores and bottoms, sand or gravel, and near offshore bars and reefs. Sunken weed beds, sharp drop-offs near rocky points, and shoals also attract it. Be sure to fish spots where rivers and streams enter a lake or reservoir.

Panfish

No matter where you live, panfish are only as far away as the nearest oversized puddle of water. "Panfish" is a name for a variety of fish which includes bluegills, crappies, and other sunfish, yellow perch, and white bass. They may not be as big as other gamefish, but for their size they put up a good fight. When it comes to fine flavor, some panfish can't be beat. They are just the right size for rolling in flour or cornmeal and throwing whole into a frying pan, hence the name "panfish."

Bluegills (members of the sunfish family) like most other panfish are schooling fish. Where you find one, you know more will be waiting to take just about any small natural bait or artificial lure offered. Finding them is a matter of locating places that provide shade, cover, and adequate food. Weed beds are ideal locations for these scrappy little fighters. Many times you will not have to go any farther than the end of a small dock in a pond or lake to find them. At noon on a hot summer day, they will often move into deeper water, returning to the shallows when the sun sets and the shadows of late afternoon lengthen. These habits may sound the same as those of the largemouth bass we have discussed. The fact is that they are the same: Many fishermen looking for small bluegills have suddenly found themselves face to face with hefty largemouth bass!

Bluegills and other sunfish have small mouths, so use small hooks and natural baits, as well as smaller artificial lures. Their natural instinct tells them to stalk a moving bait slowly and study a natural bait before deciding to strike. For this reason, artificial lures should be retrieved very slowly, and natural baits should be allowed to set still.

Since most bait fishing is done with a float, you can usually tell what is going on beneath the water and when to set your hook before pulling in your prize. The tendency is to try for the fish at the instant the float disappears for the first time; more often than not, this effort will be unrewarded. There really is no hurry, so let it pull the float under—give it a chance to enjoy its meal—then set the hook, and reel it in.

The **yellow perch** run a close second to bluegills in panfish popularity. Like the bluegills, they are not fussy about what they eat, and for bait you can use anything that is small which crawls, hops, or flies in waters where perch are found. They will even strike at a variety of spinners with attached bait. The prime perch bait, however, is a small minnow.

Perch usually prefer deeper water than do sunfish. Large perch definitely prefer the depths, so if you find yourself hooking small fish near the surface, get your bait down deeper for a real panful.

If you develop an interest in ice fishing, you'll be glad to know that yellow perch are among the most cooperative cold-weather feeders. They can normally be found around submerged brush piles and in the deep sections of a pond or lake.

When you locate a school of these golden beauties, it is not uncommon to catch enough to fill an ice chest after a day's fishing. Although they are not great fighters, their meat is flaky and makes an excellent meal. They have also been known to make avid perch fishermen out of the most casual anglers.

"Crappie" is one of dozens of local names for this large member of the sunfish family. Depending on where you live, either black crappies or white crappies

or both may be available for continuous frisky action. The black crappie has a dark back (hence the name "black crappie") and spotted sides; the "white" crappie is actually silver. Both, however, are suckers for a lively minnow but will take almost any other kind of natural bait. They usually travel in large schools, so when you locate them be prepared for action.

During the summer's heat, fish for crappies in water 15 to 20 feet deep. When they spawn in the spring or when the water temperature becomes moderate in the fall, they can be found swarming in the shallows and inlets of a lake. It is important to know that crappies feed at different levels in the water. To catch your share you'll have to discover the depth of their feeding activity at the time. This often accounts for one fisherman loading up with fish, while surrounding anglers' efforts are hopeless.

The most difficult panfish to catch are **white bass,** which are silver in color. Ranging from Canada to Texas, these fish appear as if from nowhere in large, hungry schools, and they disappear just as fast. They are cooperative after spawning in the spring and will take most natural baits and small artificial lures.

The **yellow bass,** or the striper, is the golden cousin of the white bass and is fairly common throughout the South. Its habits are similar to the white bass, and it can be taken with the same angling methods.

Trout

More has been written and discussed about trout fishing than about almost all gamefish combined. Mention this to a die-hard bass fisherman, and you had better be prepared for a long-winded debate about which is tops. We will discuss the brook and rainbow trout, which were native to American waters when the first settlers came, and the brown trout, which immigrated from Europe in 1883 and can be found today in most of our Northern States, as well as parts of Canada.

All trout prefer cool, clean waters and demand more oxygen than other species. Their most typical habitat is a cold, rushing stream in a hilly or mountainous region. In fact, some of the best trout streams are so narrow you can step across them, while others are wide and deep.

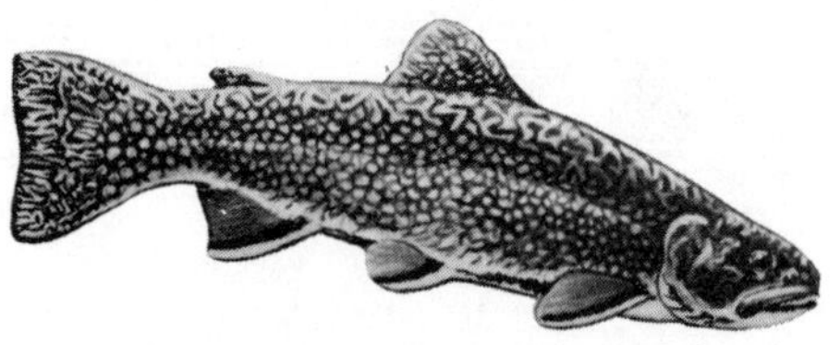

The **brook trout** (also called brookie, eastern trout, square tail, speckled trout, or native trout) is a gayly colored, speckled gamester which is popular with many anglers: It is less wary than other trout and easy to catch with either natural or artificial baits. The brookie is more sensitive than others of the species and cannot survive in waters over 70 degrees. Most brook trout average 6 to 12 inches in length, and in some large lakes and rivers, 7- to 8-pounders are not uncommon. The current record brook trout, taken from the Nipigon River in Ontario in 1916, is a whopping 14½ pounder.

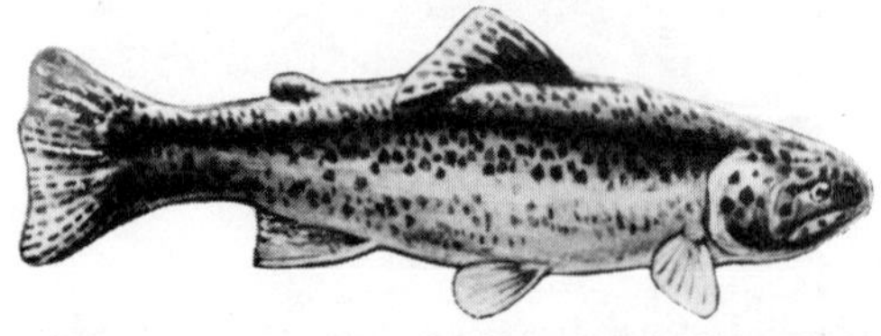

The **rainbow trout** is the rugged, leaping, thrashing sportster of the family. Originally native to the Western States, it is now found in the Northern, Eastern, and

Southern States in cool mountain streams or large rivers and lakes. In the large rivers and lakes, a 10- to 20-inch rainbow is common; 15- to 20-pounders are taken regularly in many waters; and although the rod-and-reel record is a 42-pounder, fish approaching the 50-pound mark occasionally have been reported.

Look for rainbow trout in the churning turbulence of fast-moving water as well as the deep, dark drop-offs of a lake. Use flashy spoons and spinners; colorful, gaudy flies; or a plump, round salmon egg, its favorite food, for bait.

The **brown trout,** *Salmo trutta* (genus), is the European cousin of American trout. It is the heartiest of trout, being able to withstand warmer and somewhat polluted water conditions. The brown, especially an older and larger brown, is also one of the smartest of trout. Although selective in its feeding habits, it does, however, rise eagerly for a dry fly.

As the name implies, the brown trout is usually colored a shade of brown which can range from pale, dirty yellow to olive or greenish brown. Its sides are spotted with orange or red speckles, and there are dark spots on the head, dorsal fin, and back.

The world's record brown taken from Loch Awe, Scotland, in 1866, weighed 39½ pounds. A brown may reach 40 pounds but in most waters ranges from 1 to 10 pounds.

The "brownie's" favorite waters are lakes, rivers, or streams which provide lots of grassy cover and numerous undercut banks. In fast water, you'll find a brown lying in front of a rock or boulder that splits the current.

Pike

The pickerel, northern pike, and muskellunge of the pike family are the most vicious of all our freshwater fish. At times they will strike at anything that moves in the water and will even eat each other! The giant of

the group is the **muskellunge** which is usually found in northern waters, although some are caught in Pennsylvania and as far south as Kentucky. The muskie is very wary; it has often been said that it takes an average of a thousand casts to catch one. If you've got the patience, look for this bruiser in the larger lakes and rivers that are weedy and harbor numbers of sunken logs and trees. Big baits, such as suckers and 8- to 10-inch spoons are a must when after this battler.

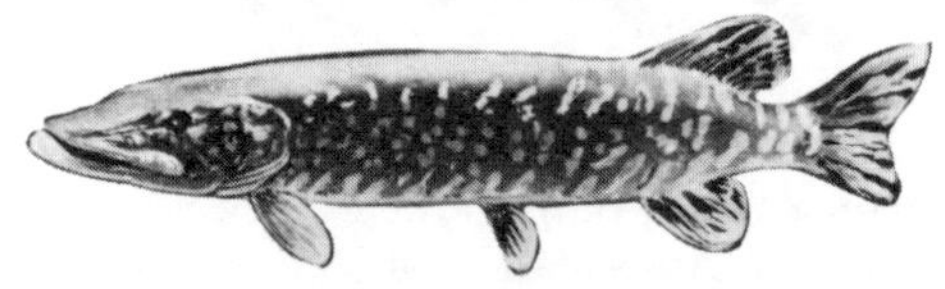

Northern pike are more plentiful than muskellunge and are easier to catch since they are found in a great range of waters. Although the average size of the pike is smaller than the muskie's (some say it reaches 100 pounds), most anglers use heavy tackle and lines up to a 30-pound test. Both muskie and pike have large mouths and plenty of sharp teeth, so be careful to use a gaff or net when lifting them from the water, and make sure you are using a wire leader when fishing for them.

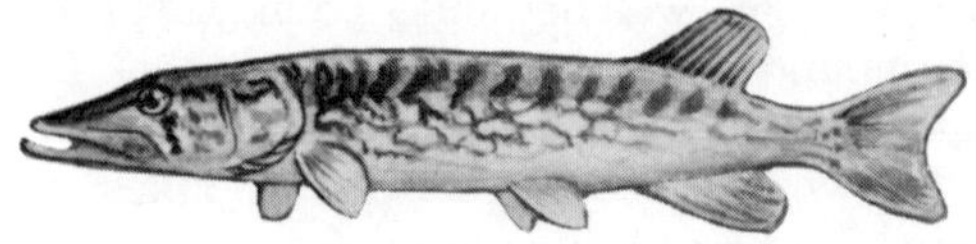

The **pickerel** is the most popular and plentiful member of the pike family. The average pickerel is 2 to 3 pounds, with a few reaching 5 pounds: Hook into one and you'll realize it's all fighter. Still-fishing with minnows is probably the most dependable angling method. If you cast with artificial lures, work them slowly but with plenty of rod action. Short, quick jerks and stop-and-go retrieves are generally most productive.

Ice Fishing

By no means let winter's icy breath freeze your spirits and enthusiasm for fishing. To a great many fishermen, fishing is at its very best during the winter months even though local lakes and streams may be frozen over. In fact, some say the fish that continue to feed regardless of the cold-water temperatures – such as pike, pickerel, walleyes, crappies, yellow perch, and bluegills – are much more flavorful than at any other time of the year.

To fish, you'll naturally need to make a hole in the ice. You'll know where to put the hole and where the fish are concentrated from day to day by reading the outdoor columns in newspapers, talking to area tackle shop owners, or simply by going out to the lake itself and finding the other fishermen. You can be sure that when one fisherman finds fish, others will start to crowd around the same spot. If there are no fishermen or signs of fishing around, try to locate likely areas where the fish would be or would feed, as you would in summertime. However, before going out on any frozen water, *make sure the ice is thick enough to support your weight* by checking with local authorities.

The simplest method of cutting through the ice is with an ice auger, which looks like a squat corkscrew with a long handle. Just screw it down through the ice, and you'll be ready to fish. Chopping your way through with an ax or chisel will leave ragged edges that can cut or fray your line. Ice fishing tools should also include a sieve or strainer of some kind to lift chips of ice out of the hole and to stir the water which turns slushy as it begins to freeze over again.

A simple hand line or lightweight tackle is enough for ice fishing. If state laws permit, you may want to use a "tip-up" which is a signal, usually a flag or bell, triggered when a fish pulls the line down. For bait, use minnows, worms, or any type of grub; just keeping the hooks baited when a school of panfish comes by is a job in itself.

Chum may be used to attract fish to your area, or sometimes other fishermen may stomp the surrounding ice to scare the fish in your direction. Another feature of ice fishing is that you don't have to worry about putting fish on a stringer when there is action: Just drop them on the ice, and they'll be quick-frozen and remain fresh until the day is over.

It is most important for any winter sport to prepare to be warm and dry. The wrong time to wish you had dressed more warmly is when you are out in the middle of a lake and the fish are just starting to bite. Dress with layers of clothing rather than with a few heavy, bulky clothes. Earmuffs, gloves, and sunglasses to protect your eyes from glare are a must. Above all, be sure to protect your feet with warm socks and insulated overshoes.

Many veteran ice fishermen build shanties measuring 4 by 4 by 6 feet and mount them on sled runners for easy towing from place to place. An ice shanty provides shelter from cold winds and may have all the comforts of home if stocked with a portable stove and reading material or a radio to pass the time till the fish bite. Of course, a simple windbreak of canvas or plywood constructed in a V-shape will provide shelter, if not entertainment.

Saltwater Fishing

The sea holds a mysterious attraction for fishermen. It's hard to know whether the early morning cries of sea gulls, the whispering hiss of a foam-laced beach, the salted spray of crashing breakers, or the endless mission to hook the big one is what lures surf casters, time after time, to King Neptune's salty lair.

A breed unlike any other, surf casters roam the most desolate stretches of beach in search of clues to the presence of their prey. These lonely hunters can be spotted working the beaches and jetties from the time the first dogwood blooms until the bitter cold nights ice their lines and lures. They know that eventually they will be at the right place at the right time: the moment a big fish comes chasing its food across the shallows of a receding tide or lies in wait within their reach in a channel or near a rocky point. The surf fishermen's grounds stretch out in endless miles along our country's coast.

The Lure of the Surf

Crashing breakers, flying spray, and the hiss of spreading foam mark the battleground where the hunter and the hunted meet. This is surf country where the sandbars, channels, riptides, and sloughs trap bait that draw the attention of game fish and angler alike.

The variety of prizes available depends largely on the area you are fishing. The gamut of fish runs through blues, striped bass, channel bass, and flounder; in size, from 1 to over 100 pounds! A long-handled surf rod provides the leverage needed to throw your bait well out beyond the breakers. A spinning or revolving-spool reel is loaded with at least 200 yards of heavy line in case your fish decides to make a long, fast run.

Successful surf casters have learned to read a beach, recognize the signs that point to fish. They will often walk a stretch of beach at low tide studying and looking for sandbars, rocks, and gullies that are normally covered when the tide rises. They know that these places are where fish will congregate and where the action of rolling water will tumble bait and break up shellfish as natural bait.

Big fish will chase bait up to the beach if they have to or feed in the trough created by a receding wave. Veterans will watch the waveline along the beach looking for the spot where the water climbs highest onto the sand indicating deep holes. They'll watch the height of incoming waves, because they know that waves begin to break when the depth of the water equals the height of the rollers.

In some parts of the country, rocky jetties extend seaward from the beach. These natural or, in some cases, man-made breakwaters generally provide consistent fishing. Most game fish gather around jetties, because baitfish seek protection there. Experienced jetty jockeys will work the pockets formed between the jetty and the beach. However, they also know that, while the fishing may be good, they have to constantly be on guard for slippery, algae-coated rocks. These can be treacherous when the seas are high, and some, tough going at all times.

Bottom Fishing

Fishing with bait at or near the bottom of any body of saltwater is the most popular method of catching fish. Perhaps the reason is that at one time or another almost every type of fish feeds on the bottom. The technique is easy; the variety of fish caught is great; and it provides hours of enjoyment at little or no cost.

Wherever you find a bridge of any sort over water, you'll usually find fishermen. In fact, some piers are built specially for fishermen, and a fee may be charged to fish from them. Tackle at places like these is rarely a consideration for enticing fish – just about anything goes. Whether fishing from a party boat, pier, bridge, or causeway, the object is simply to get the bait to the fish by dropping it straight down. Also of prime importance is a line strong enough to haul the fish in and, if possible, a heavy sinker to overcome currents and get the bait to the bottom.

To some, bottom fishing is nothing more than waiting for a fish to strike. Others delight in experimenting with new riggings, baits, and techniques. Many anglers use a method called live-line fishing when a strong current is present: They use a light sinker or no sinker at all and let the bait drift naturally. Veteran fishermen carefully calculate every one of their moves – and their results usually are more fish. They check their bait often and replace it if it seems worn. You can also try different sinker weights or change the hook size. Periodic movement of the rig along the bottom at times will make a difference.

When the tide is low, study the waters surrounding bridges and piers. Under and around them, much as in a bass lake, certain spots are more to the liking of fish than others as they wait for food to swim or be carried by in the currents. It is often possible to locate groups of resting fish at low tide and successfully fish these areas when the tide returns. Some of the bottom feeders are notorious bait stealers, and the angler must have a steady hand and concentration to hook them at the right moment. Bottom fishing can provide exciting sport.

Surf-Casting Techniques

The basic techniques of surf casting are not unlike the reel-handling methods described in the "Spinning" and "Bait Casting" sections of this book. The equipment is much the same except that every piece of tackle designed for saltwater is usually built on a larger scale: Reels are huskier; rods can measure from 8 to 11 feet long; and lines and lures are made heavier.

The preparatory casting steps are the same as the ready-to-cast positions for the spinning and bait-casting reels (reviewed earlier); they are illustrated here as a reminder. The lure or terminal tackle should be reeled in to within 12 to 16 inches of the rod tip. If you are casting with a bait-casting reel, be sure to push the click button to the off position and depress the free-spool button prior to casting.

In your final preparation for surf casting, grip the butt of the rod at a comfortable distance below the reel. If you are right-handed, extend your left foot out in front of the right one and point it in the direction of the target area. The cast will arc the rod over your right shoulder. If you are left-handed, the rod will be over your left shoulder with the right foot leading.

Let's go over the ready position, shown at right: Point your leading foot toward the target area; hold the rod at shoulder level and point it in the opposite direction, placing your weight on the rear foot; and before casting, look behind you to make sure the hooks on your line

are clear of obstructions and that anyone standing around is at a safe distance.

Begin the cast with gradually increasing speed. Swing the rod tip up by pulling the rod butt toward your chest and pushing the reel away from you at the same time. Your shoulders and hips should pivot forward as your weight is shifted from your rear foot to the leading foot. The most important factor of a good cast is a smooth and steady increase in speed.

As the rod butt reaches the vertical position (pointing at 6 o'clock) the rod tip will be pulling the terminal tackle at maximum speed. Now is the time to release the line while you continue to pull the rod tip forward: The lure will be on its way like a shot! Timing is all important and can be conquered only with practice. Soon, this casting method will become second nature. As you become better, you'll take pride in each cast. If at first the lure follows a high arcing path, you'll know the line was released too soon. However, the lure will splash into the water at your feet if you wait too long to release the line. See illustrations above.

Natural Baits for Saltwater

There is no substitute for the real thing, and natural

baits are exactly that. In most cases, if it is the natural food of the fish you are after, most of the time they will take it. Of course, the kind of bait varies in different areas, but the techniques outlined here will generally remain the same.

You can usually get good advice from bait dealers on the best baits to use. Their job is to obtain bait daily and then sell it to anglers, who provide updated information on the fishing action. Although smart anglers use more than one bait if they expect to make good catches, certain baits do produce consistent results with certain types of fish.

Sea worms (also known as clam worms or sandworms) are excellent for bottom-feeding fish of all kinds. They may also be trolled behind a boat or allowed to drift free in a current for surface or mid-depth feeders such as stripers or weakfish. Normally, you can dig them up yourself from the muddy sand of tidal flats or look for them under rocks alongshore at low tide.

Bloodworms are quite similar to sea worms and can be found in the same places. Both can be kept alive for a few days if kept cool in a container with moist seaweed. For longer storage periods, keep them on ice or in a refrigerator. Stir them every now and then to keep them separated; otherwise, they become tangled in the bottom of the container and sometimes eat each other.

When baited for larger fish, hook them in the tough skin just below the head and let their long bodies trail

NATURAL BAITS

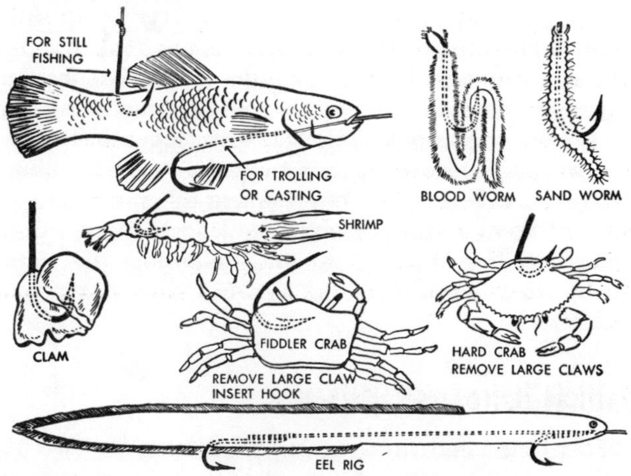

behind the hook. Use small sections of the worm when after small bottom feeders.

Clams, which can be found on mudflats and low-tide areas, are also good natural baits. They can be kept alive and fresh for short periods on ice. For longer periods of time, it is best to put them in a container and keep them in the water. The strong muscular foot of the clam is tough and will stay on a hook very well. For some fish, cut the clam meat up in small pieces; for others, remove the meat from the shell, wrap it in a small-mesh bag, and tie it on a hook.

Squid is also very popular for taking many kinds of fish. A small squid used whole makes a great trolling bait, while the larger ones may be cut into strips. Cut baits should be shaped triangularly with a split tail so that they wiggle in the water. They can also be used with feathered jigs, spoons, and spinners as an added attraction to fish.

Fresh shrimp is the most popular bait of surf, jetty, pier, and bridge fishermen in Florida and along the gulf coast. Although it doesn't necessarily have to be alive, it should be as fresh as possible. The reason is simple: They thrive in these waters and almost all the gulf species (including weakfish, flounder, redfish, small black drum, whiting, and snook) quite often feed only on shrimp. If you use them while they are alive, hook them through the tail to keep them active. Dead shrimp will appear alive if hooked in the same manner and trailed through the water; or cut a large one into pieces and use it for bottom fishing.

In addition to the baits listed above, various saltwater fish make excellent bait for other fish. The hardy saltwater killie, often called a minnow, is one that may be used as a live bait. The same is true of eels. Menhaden caught in abundance by commercial fishermen and processed for their oils work well when cut into chunks. Also in this category include butterfish, herring, bluefish, and mackerel, for they too are oily fish that as bait will leave a slick, or smell trail, in the water that attracts feeding fish. In general, determine the right bait by what is available and by what kind of fish you are after.

Artificial Lures for Saltwater

Most lures used in saltwater fishing can be used in

freshwater as well, so it would not make much sense to draw a definite line between the two. If most fishermen had to make a general statement as to the difference, they would say that in some situations artificial lures used for saltwater fishing are larger, although even the smallest freshwater lures are a must to catch some saltwater fish. Since we have already given a brief history and description of artificial lures in the freshwater section, let's take a look at some of the lures for saltwater and how they are used.

Tube lures are saltwater trolling and jigging lures made from rubber or plastic tubing. (See illustration.) Single tubes, which can vary in length, usually have a built-in curve and imitate an eel in the water. Multiple tube rigs, often called umbrella rigs, attract many kinds of game fish by simulating an entire school of baitfish. These are not meant to be jigged but rather trolled at a steady rate at the depth of the feeding fish. A string of short tubes can be used with a heavyweight diamond jig to imitate a school of shiners as the jig is worked up and down in deep water.

Both poppers and stick baits are classified as surface plugs and are available in a large variety of sizes for both freshwater and saltwater use. The popper produces a splashing, popping surface-disturbing commotion when reeled in rapidly with an occasional twitch of the rod tip. Stick baits are more streamlined than these blunt-nosed poppers. When they are retrieved, stick baits wag back and forth.

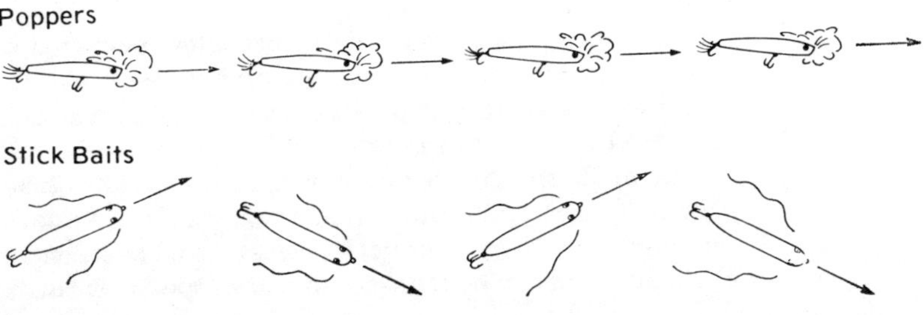

Sinking swimmers are lures that sink and swim, just as the name implies. They are mid-depth plugs and can be fished at any level by letting them go down until they reach the desired depth. Work them in the same manner as the other subsurface plugs described earlier.

Sinking Swimmers

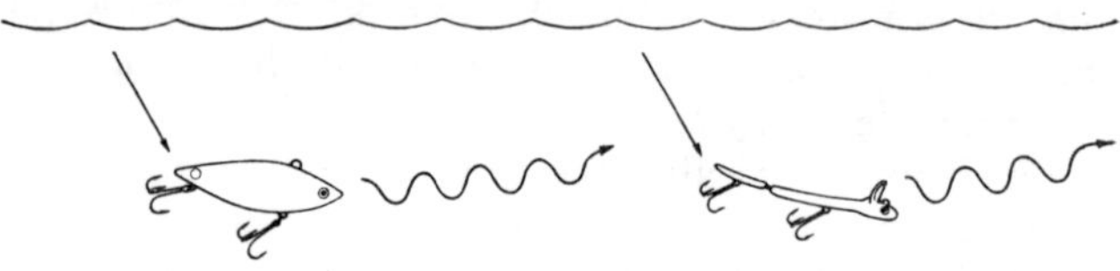

The soft plastic lures are designed to imitate not only the appearance but also the fleshy softness and natural movement of a live bait. The Plastic Eel, for example, will fool many a fish by the way it looks and by its eel-like movement. These lures are used primarily for casting and trolling in saltwater. They are most effective when retrieved at a moderate, steady rate of speed.

Soft Plastic Lures

Care of Saltwater Tackle

All fishing equipment needs special care (cleaning, oiling, and repair) to continue to serve its purpose. It is most important with saltwater tackle, because sand and salt combine to corrode tackle if it is not cared for. Although most saltwater equipment is manufactured from materials which can withstand much of the corrosive exposure from seaside use, special cleaning and oiling is constantly necessary to keep this equipment in good shape after each trip.

Removing salt and sand takes only a few moments if your tackle has not been neglected. After every outing, it is always a good idea to rinse everything – rod, reel, lures, and hooks – in freshwater. Wipe them clean, and dry them thoroughly before storing. Periodically, take your reel apart and clean, oil, and regrease it to remove sand and grit. Keep your hooks cleaned and sharpened. Nicks in a rod can be touched up with a spot of varnish.

Saltwater Fish

Striped Bass

When the striped bass are in, you'll see fishermen running for their tackle along the Atlantic coast from North Carolina to Maine and from California to Oregon on the Pacific. This bass is a tireless fighter, and there are few fish in all the seas that can compare to it either on the end of a line or on the table.

During their spring run, stripers can be taken in the marshes and inlets and back in the tidal streams when they begin to spawn. Sometimes they'll travel in

schools of thousands, usually weighing under 5 pounds, but don't be surprised if you find yourself battling one over 10 or 25 pounds. In the surf, striped bass can be found feeding on the incoming tides or lying in the deep-water channels just offshore when the tide is out.

Trolling is a very effective method of covering a lot of known striper water for a day of fishing. Many anglers find live-line fishing quite effective as they drift along in a current: Using no weights on the line, they add natural action to their bait. When surf casting for stripers, just about anything goes from natural bait to artificial lures. In general, striped bass have been known to be a bit fussy about what they eat, but anything other fish will eat or hit will at one time or another be interesting to striped bass.

Weakfish

When anglers set hooks into their first weakfish (sea trout), they are usually quite surprised when the fish does not live up to its name. A surface lure may be hit with a shattering jolt. If you become overenthusiastic and set the hook too hard, you'll find the weakfish gets its name from its fragile mouth.

Weakfish are also known as yellowfin and squeteague in some areas. They are popular with fishermen all along the Atlantic coast and down into the gulf region. Whether bottom fishing, trolling, live-line fishing, or just surf casting with natural baits and artificial lures, once one has struck, play it carefully to avoid ripping the hook free as it makes repeated runs for freedom. Maintain tension on the line at all times because if you give a weakfish enough slack, it will throw your bare hook right back at you!

Most of the weakfish food supply consists of minnows and shrimp, but they also take worms, squid, and other baits. Since they feed at various levels, try the surf rigs illustrated on page 56, when fishing with natural bait.

California Yellowtail

This member of the amberjack family is usually known by the name yellowtail but may often be confused with other fish referred to by that same name. The California yellowtail is most common on the Pacific coast from Los Angeles County to the tip of Baja, Calif. Fishermen in this area find that casting live sardines or anchovies is a very good method of hooking into a 5- to 30-pound bundle of aquatic muscle. Once a yellowfish feels the sting of a hook, its actions are wild and furious. At times, the battle will be a thrashing surface display while, at others, the yellowtail may go down deep and bullishly refuse to come to the surface. When you finally wear out a yellowtail and bring it to the boat, it is not unusual to see several others following, curious as to the cause of the recent commotion.

Channel Bass

Depending on who's talking the loudest, channel bass may also be called redfish, red drum, drum, or red bass even though they are not really bass but are related to a family of fish called croakers. Nevertheless, they are one of the finest game fish found in American waters ranging from North Carolina southward. When feeding in the surf, they may chase baitfish so close to shore that these 20- to 40-pound bulls can be seen in water so shallow that their backs are exposed.

Ordinarily, channel bass are bottom feeders that spend their time leisurely searching for crabs and other bottom food. Although they may give the impression of being rather sluggish fish, as soon as they feel the point of a hook bite deep, they'll be off in a surge that'll make your reel drag scream for mercy. Make sure you've got line testing at least 30 pounds and plenty of it!

Bluefish

Blues can provide some of the most exciting fishing you'll find anywhere. When a large school hits a stretch of beach, it is not strange to see the water "boil" and to witness the sea turn red as they cut a path of merciless destruction through schools of baitfish. In fact, during such a feeding frenzy, it would not be uncommon for a bluefish to eat until it is stuffed, throw up all it has already eaten, and begin again. While the smaller blues are attacking bait, another school of larger ones will frequently start feeding on the small bluefish!

Bluefish are unique fish, and their characteristics make them the greatest fighting fish for their size in all the seven seas. When you locate a pack of them feeding, it makes little difference what lure you use as long as you keep it moving as fast as you can. At times, blues can be caught in the surf, but the most popular method is trolling since the schools are constantly traveling. Some fishermen chum them by throwing quantities of ground-up menhaden or other baitfish into the water to drift with the currents. Feeding blues are attracted to the drifting slick and will follow it right up to its source. As long as the chum holds out, blues can be taken all around the boat until your arms feel so tired from the strain that you feel they may fall off.

When fishing blues always use a wire or very heavy monofilament leader. Their aggressive feeding habits have provided them with very sharp teeth that will easily cut through any standard line. They range in size from 1-pound snappers to 30-pound bulls.

Flounder

The flounder belongs to a family called flatfish. Although there are more than 200 different types, the most common in the northeast and mid-Atlantic are the summer flounder (called fluke) and the winter flounder.

Summer flounders live in the sandy- and muddy-bottomed shallow waters of the Atlantic seaboard from Cape Cod to Georgia. By nature, they are very curious fish and will tend to investigate any silvery or flashing movement. They will suck the object into their mouth and quickly spit it out if it doesn't taste good; so if you fish the fluke with artificial lures, strike the moment you feel the slightest movement out of the ordinary.

Winter flounder can be caught from piers, docks, beaches, or a boat drifting alongshore. Once the fish are located, they may actually carpet the bottom. Fish for flounders at high tide on sand flats or soft, rich, black mud bottoms, especially if shrimp, crabs, etc., are available.

Salmon

Salmon belong to the same family as the trout. **Pacific salmon** are born in many of the freshwater inland streams from California to Alaska; they migrate into the open seas where they grow to maturity and then eventually return to the stream of their birth to spawn and finally die. The best fishing for this type of salmon occurs when they gather at the mouths of rivers where they feed like mad for the last time getting ready for their long upstream journey to spawn. At these times, the most popular method of fishing for them is trolling with heavy tackle and live herring, sardines, or anchovies. Occasionally, they are taken on spoons or plugs.

Atlantic salmon, unlike their Pacific cousin, may spawn more than once. Sport fishermen consider them one of the best fish to catch because of their powerful ability to fight and leap—at times 5 or 6 feet into the air! Even after they have migrated upstream, they will continue to take spoons, plugs, or live bait. However, the Atlantic salmon is best known to the fly-fisherman; for in many areas, fly-fishing is the only legal method of taking them.

Terminal Rigs for Saltwater Fishing

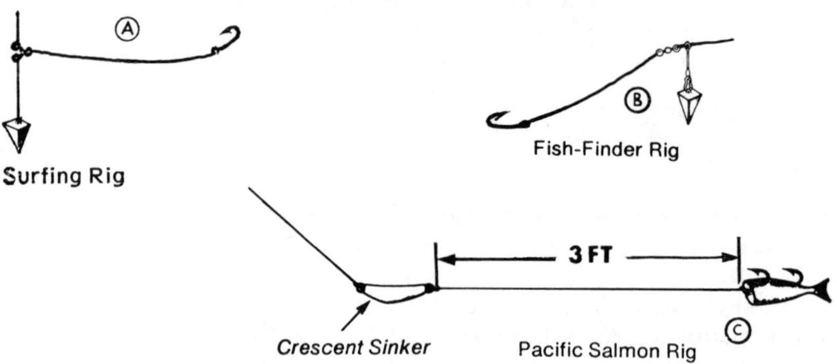

Surf Rigs

Surf anglers generally use two basic rigs when fishing with natural baits. The first, the standard surf rig (illustration A), makes use of a three-way swivel. The swivel is tied a few inches above a pyramid sinker. The hook and leader are tied to one eye on the three-way swivel, and the line is attached to the remaining eye.

The other rig is known as the fish-finder rig (illustration B). The fish-finder has a ring on one end and a snap on the other. A large-sized snap swivel may be used as a substitute. A barrel swivel is inserted between the leader and the line to act as a stop.

Both rigs can be used with different length leaders and various sizes and types of hooks, depending on the fish you are after. Nylon monofilament, wire, or stainless-steel wire measuring about 18 inches long is recommended. Either rig can be used for striped bass, channel bass, blues, weakfish, and other surf-feeding fish.

Pacific Salmon Rig

This is an ideal rig for slow trolling or drifting when fishing for king and coho salmon. A plug-cut or a whole herring is attached to a two-hook rig on a 3-foot leader. The leader is attached to the eye of a crescent sinker

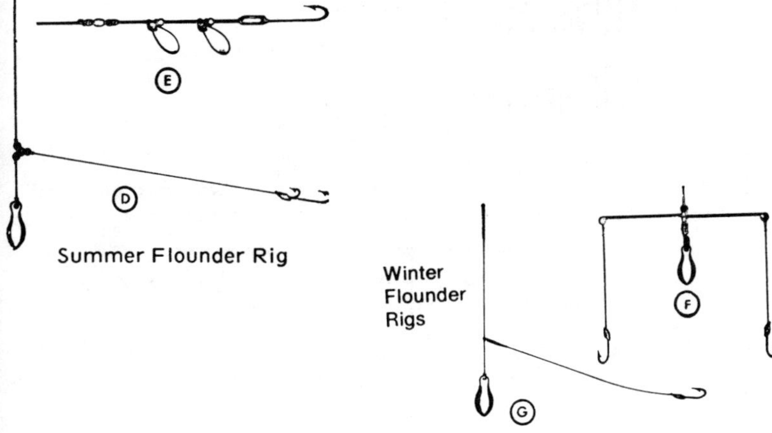

weighing from 2 to 6 ounces depending on the current and depth you want to fish. Let the rig go down to the bottom, and then reel back slowly. When you get your first strike, mark your line so you can let the rig down to the same depth again (illustration C).

Summer Flounder Rig

To rig for fluke (illustration D), attach 2 or 3 feet of leader to one eye of a three-way swivel. Attach a sinker to another eye with only an inch or two of leader line. Then, attach a long-shanked hook to the end of the leader. Use a strip of squid or clam for bait. To further enhance the rig and draw the attention of more fish, add a spinner blade or two to the leader (illustration E).

Winter Flounder Rigs

The two-hooked rig (illustration F) uses a wire spreader to keep the two hooks apart so that they can lie together on the bottom where the flounder will be feeding. The sinker is attached to a snap in the middle. The single-hooked rig (illustration G) has its hook tied a few inches above the sinker. Both rigs use a long-shanked hook.

How To Clean Fish

Fish taste best if they can be eaten soon after they are caught. They should be kept alive, if possible, until they are cleaned, and then if they cannot be eaten immediately, the cleaned fish should be placed on ice or in a freezer. A fish's flavor perishes quickly. You'll find, too, that fresh fish are easiest to scale.

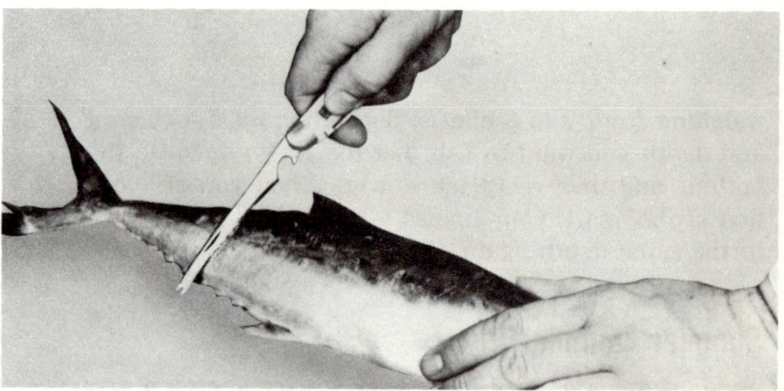

First, scale the fish. Use a knife with a special saw-toothed scaling edge or regular knife blade. Scrape from tail to head.

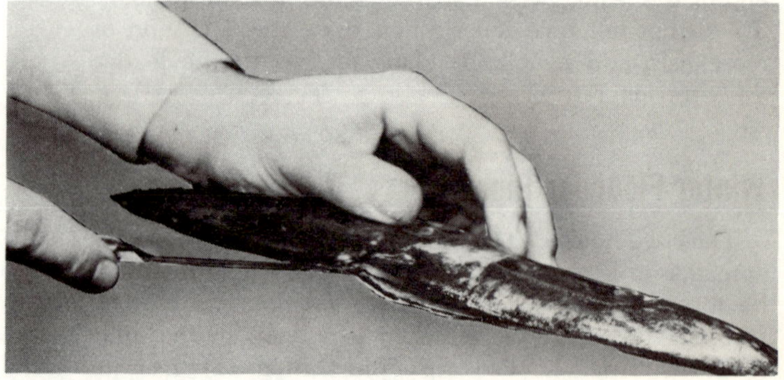

Next, remove dorsal fin and belly fin. Run tip of the knife along each side of fin and lift it out—with bones attached.

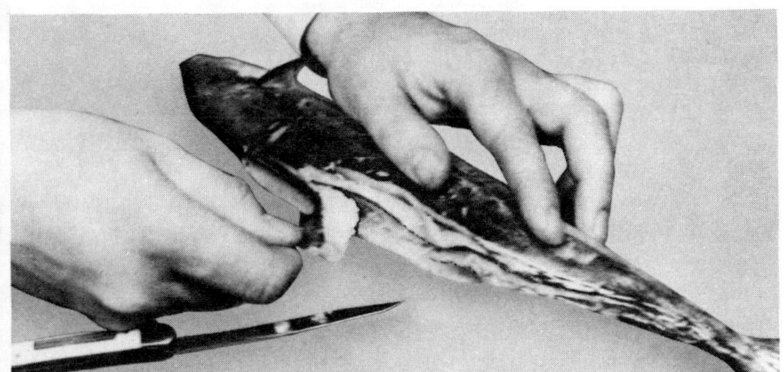

Note small bones removed with fins. If the fins are cut off with knife instead of lifted out, these bones remain in the fish.

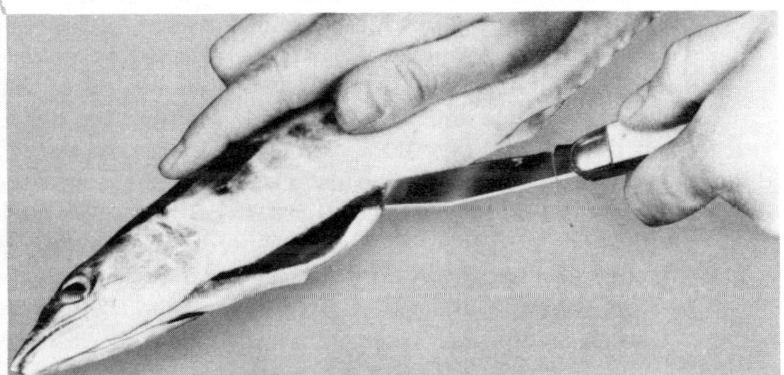

Gut the fish by making a slit from throat to vent. Strip the entrails from cavity with fingers, then wash it out thoroughly.

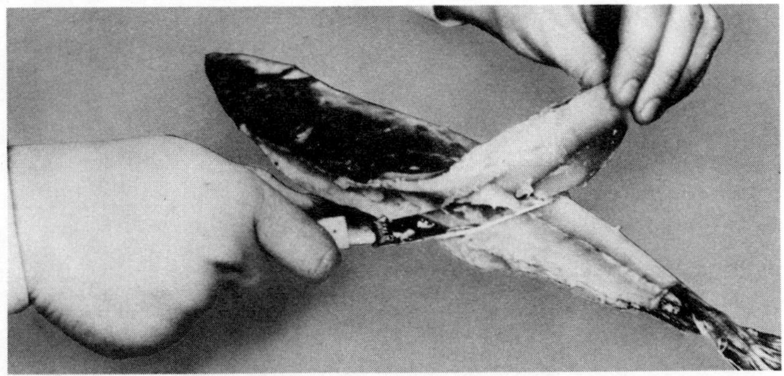

You can filet fish by slicing along each side close to backbone from tail to head. This results in two boneless pieces of fish.

The Future of Fishing

A few years ago fishing was becoming steadily worse everywhere. Until recently, in fact, many laws were passed every year reducing the number of days you could go fishing and the number of fish you could catch. This divided up the dwindling supply of fish but did nothing to improve the fishing.

A lot is being done now to make the fishing better. In many places, of course, fishing is still bad and is becoming worse. Generally, though, it is improving, and here's why.

As more and more people became interested in sport fishing, they wanted to know how fishing could be made better again. Many remedies were tried but failed. Then trained biologists were asked to help.

The biologists studied the living conditions of fish in our streams and lakes. They also studied the habits of the fish and how they reproduce. They soon learned that in many places the fishing was poor because the fish could no longer live in the water. Cities had grown up along streambanks and lakeshores where once before there had been only forests and prairies. Sewage from the cities and pollution from their industries were dumped into the water. Often it killed the fish by poisoning them, or it destroyed their food or eliminated their supply of oxygen.

Farmers were as guilty as the city dwellers. They tried to raise crops on every foot of their farms, and so they cleared away the forests and the grasslands. They

laid their land bare, and some of it washed away with every rain. Streams which had once flowed steadily because the water wasn't held back by the soil and by the roots of plants began to flood when it rained and to become dry in between times. Fine dirt, called silt, washed out of the fields and settled over the bottoms of streams and lakes. It covered the sand and gravel beds where the fish had laid their eggs, and it reduced the amount of available oxygen. Cold-water streams were no longer shaded by overhanging trees nor fed by cold springs or underground seepage. Their waters became too warm for certain kinds of fish.

When the land became poor (its rich topsoil washed away), the water became poor, too. The food which fish feed on must grow in rich water, and the water depends upon the land around it for its nutrition. Fish could not grow abundantly where there was not enough food for them, and almost everywhere, the places where fish lived were being destroyed or changed.

Many things are being done today to correct these conditions. Fish biologists have stopped most of the expensive and wasteful stocking of fish in waters where the fish cannot reproduce. They have made more space for game fish, like bass and trout, by seining or chemically treating certain fishing waters to get rid of overabundant panfish or undesirable rough fish such as carp and suckers. Cities are cooperating by treating their sewage; industries are purifying their wastes; farmers are holding their soil on the land. The number of clean places for fish to live in is increasing.

Sport fishermen helped bring about the change: They cooperated with the biologists in getting most of the laws restricting fishing removed. In most states, you can now catch many kinds of fish all times of year. There is no limit on the number or size. In some places, of course, it still seems best to have some regulations. In other places, the stocking of fish is yet unharmful. Wherever the biologists have been permitted to work, the fishing has grown steadily better.

You can help improve fishing where you live. Get acquainted with your fish and game protector and the fish conservation people in your area. Take part in their programs. Study the fishing conditions in the lakes and streams where you fish and learn what you can do to make them better.

More Information on Fishing

The Garcia Corporation offers an exclusive collection of paperback books covering many of today's most popular types of fishing. Each one includes important tips, tricks, and skills. They are written and edited by many of North America's most famous sportsmen. These books are sold by local tackle shops or can be ordered directly from the Garcia Corporation, 329 Alfred Ave., Teaneck, N.J. 07666. If ordered, please send remittance including state and local tax if applicable. (Prices are subject to change without notice.)

Garcia Fishing Library ($1.25 ea.)

Freshwater Skills in Saltwater, Mark Sosin, Code 69001
Pan Fishing, Mark Sosin, Code 69002
Shark Fishing, Mark Sosin, Code 69003
Rig Trolling Baits, Mark Sosin, Code 69004
Artificial Lures, Mark Sosin, Code 69005
Largemouth Bass, Milt Rosko, Code 69007
Surf Fishing, Milt Rosko, Code 69008
Party Boat Fishing, Milt Rosko, Code 69009
Freshwater Fishing, Milt Rosko, Code 69010
Fly-Fishing, Lefty Kreh, Code 69011
Tips and Tricks of Spinning, Lefty Kreh, Code 69012
Trout, Howard Brant, Code 69013
Basic Bottom Rigs, Vlad Evanoff, Code 69014
Backpacking, G. A. Cunningham, Code 69600
Better Casting, Ann Strobel and Joan Salvato Wulff
Walleye, Pike, Musky, and Pickerel, L. James Bashline, Code 69015
How To Catch Coho, Jerry Chiapetta, Code 69016
Electronic Fishing Aids, Al Reinfelder
Fishermen's Guide to Small Boats, Jim Martenhoff, Code 69017
Worming and Plugging for Bass, Homer Circle, Code 69006

Other Books on Fishing

Check your tackle shop, bookstore, or local library to obtain copies of these books:

Fishing Across North America, Joe Brooks. Harper and Row, 10 East 53rd Street, New York, N.Y. 10022.

Fishing Tackle and Techniques, Dick Wolff. E. P. Dutton & Co., Inc., New York, N.Y. 10003.

McClane's Standard Fishing Encyclopedia, A. J. McClane. Holt, Rinehart & Winston, Inc., New York, N.Y. 10017.

Practical Fishing Knots, Lefty Kreh and Mark Sosin. Crown Publishers, Inc., 419 Park Avenue South, New York, N.Y. 10016.

Through the Fish's Eye, M. Sosin and J. Clark. Harper and Row, 10 East 53rd Street, New York, N.Y. 10022.

Acknowledgments

The Boy Scouts of America is grateful to the Garcia Corporation for editorial and technical assistance in preparing this pamphlet. Special thanks to Paul N. Jones, Executive Secretary, American Fly Casting Association, for his cooperation.

Illustration Credits

American Fly Casting Association—page 31

Joel Arrington—pages 8, 44, 48

Environmental Protection Agency—page 60

Garcia Corporation—pages 3, 9, 10, 12, 13, 14, 17, 18, 19, 20, 21, 22, 23, 24, 25, 26, 27, 28, 29, 30, 32, 34, 43, 45, 46, 49, 50, 56, 57

Mark J. Sosin—pages 4, 42

NOTES